T0265852

THE POMEGRANATE PRINCIPLE

RORY E. VERRETT WITH
PETER M. BIRKELAND

THE
POMEGRANATE
PRINCIPLE

BEST PRACTICES

IN DIVERSITY

RECRUITING

WILEY

Published by John Wiley & Sons, Inc., Hoboken, New Jersey.
Published simultaneously in Canada.

For general information on our other products and services or for technical support, please contact our Customer Care Department within the United States at (800) 762-2974, outside the United States at (317) 572-3993 or fax (317) 572-4002.

Wiley also publishes its books in a variety of electronic formats. Some content that appears in print may not be available in electronic formats. For more information about Wiley products, visit our web site at www.wiley.com.

Library of Congress Cataloging-in-Publication Data is Available:
ISBN 9781394209330 (Cloth)
ISBN 9781394209354 (ePDF)
ISBN 9781394209347 (ePub)

COVER DESIGN: PAUL MCCARTHY
COVER ART: © GETTY IMAGES | DORIN VLADU / 500PX

SKY10057595_101623

*For Louis, James, Johanna, Brenda, Karen, and Victor,
and all of the first-generation big-time leaders I've had the privilege
to mentor, coach, and recruit.*

CONTENTS

FOREWORD

On February 22, 2021, Seattle Mariners president and CEO Kevin Mather resigned from his post after inappropriate comments he made at a Rotary Club event earlier in the month went public. By March 2, I was meeting with owners, Mariners employees, and community members to discuss finding the Mariners' next leader.

When John Stanton, chairman of the Mariners, asked me to be the chair of the selection committee, I had one request: I wanted to take an approach that would build in fresh perspectives and nontraditional methods.

Enter Rory Verrett and Protégé Search.

We interviewed several national search firms, but we chose to partner with Rory because he has an impressive track record of building inclusive search processes that yield diverse candidate pools. What I find especially unique is Rory's expansive view of diversity, equity, and inclusion practices. He not only creates diverse slates of candidates, but he also helps cultivate a sense of belonging. Throughout the search process for the Mariners, Rory made concerted efforts to support candidates, and the search committee members, to bring their full selves and talents to the process. Rory emphasized to us that it was not only about diversity in demographics—but also diversity in thought and approach. Throughout the search process, Rory pushed us to think about how candidates could add value to the organization's culture and environment and vice versa. He helped us go beyond the surface level and assess what it means to create and foster a sense of belonging to enable an organization to live into its values at every level.

This was not the first national search process I've chaired in my career. During my 27-year career at Microsoft, my time as CEO at the Gates Foundation, and my tenure as the chair of Stanford's Board of Directors, I have recruited and hired many talented leaders, including technical experts, division leaders, and the president of Stanford University. Throughout these experiences, as a white, cis-gender man, it was important for me to first recognize my privilege in having a seat at the table and second, figure out ways to break out of the common molds of talent that companies and leaders were used to recruiting so that people without built-in access could access the same opportunities.

The Pomegranate Principle is a book for all hiring managers to understand how to recruit and retain exceptional, diverse talent. If I had this playbook at the start of my career, I would have led better search processes.

Throughout these pages, Rory shares a framework that unpacks how we all can identify and overcome our biases to make excellent talent selections that will improve organizational culture and outcomes. He'll walk you through five best practices that will support from beginning to end—initially through building strong pipelines of talent to setting up new leaders for success with robust onboarding support.

When I was in early conversations with search firms for the Mariners, Rory said Protégé Search was a "game-changing firm, for game-changing brands, for game-changing leaders."

He was right.

I know you'll benefit from Rory's approaches and perspectives. We all need support to build organizations that cultivate and lift up leaders from all backgrounds and talents. Diversifying whom we're learning from, following, and supporting is critical to building the inclusive economy and multi-racial democracy that everyone needs to thrive.

Jeff Raikes

Co-founder, Raikes Foundation

June 21, 2023

ACKNOWLEDGMENTS

Like a lot of books, *The Pomegranate Principle: Best Practices in Diversity Recruiting* was many years in the making. I've learned so much from my fellow diversity, equity, and inclusion, and human capital leaders working hard every day to make companies and organizations more innovative, more modern, and more meritocratic.

There are too many people to name here, but brilliant mentors and friends have been extraordinarily helpful in my career. People like Ben Wilson, the former chairman of Beveridge & Diamond law firm; Pamela Mitchell, my executive coach and the founder of The Reinvention Institute; Deb Elam, the former president of the GE Foundation and GE's Chief Diversity Officer; Jacqui Welch, the Chief Human Resources Officer at The New York Times Company; Ray Anderson, Athletic Director at Arizona State University; Robert Raben, the founder of The Raben Group; Valerie Williams, the founder of Converge Firm; David Sutphen, the founder of Jasper Advisors; Alicin Reidy Williamson, Chief Diversity and Culture Officer at Yahoo!; Lisa M. Coleman, SVP, Global Inclusion and Strategic Innovation at New York University; Kali Jones, diplomat and former Chief of Staff to the U.S. Ambassador to the United Nations; Steven J. Brooks, VP, corporate procurement at Intercontinental Hotel Group; Jeffrey P. May, principal at International Development and Planning; Jay Augustine, senior pastor of St. Joseph AME Church; Victor R. Scott, II, Chief Communications Officer at Cardinal Health; Heath Butler, partner at Mercury Fund; Robert

E. James, II, chairman of The National Bankers Association; and last, but not least, Willie J. Epps, Jr., U.S. Magistrate Judge for the Western District of Missouri. All of these brilliant souls have impacted my life in ways too extraordinary to measure. I know I'm a better person and a better leader because of the wisdom, insight, and encouragement they've poured into my mind and soul. I love you all.

I also have the greatest academy for learning about diversity, equity, and inclusion as the founder of Protégé Search, the firm I launched in 2016. I have four traits I look for with the folks we ask to join our little adventure at the firm, and those are a relentless commitment to excellence; a servant-leader ethos; a steadfast integrity; and a humanistic balance to work and life. I wish our clients could hear how we talk about them behind their backs—imagining, strategizing, and creative problem solving long after the search update calls have ended. This group of nine consultants is simply the finest group of professionals I've ever had the privilege to work with. One of the proudest achievements in my career is the fact that we've never had anyone leave the firm for another opportunity. To Sheena Simmons, Jin Liu, Anthony Marrero, D'Karla Davis, Hae Yoon, Justin Payton, Mark Kahn, and Amir Grice, thank you for sharing your brilliance in this movement to make the workplace more diverse, equitable, and inclusive. I love you all.

My family played a gigantic role in helping to steward this dream of writing a book into actually completing the process of writing it. I've hosted and edited over 200 podcast episodes, but writing a book was so much more difficult. I'm an extrovert at heart, so it's easy to invite one of my superbly accomplished friends to talk career strategy 200 times over. It's an entirely different scenario to stare at a computer screen and hope the words come out the way you think of them. Even as a former English major, I struggled on many days to get anything out.

The person who helped me the most was my wife, Tammie, who was born with an excess of patience, intelligence, integrity, compassion, and beauty. And after spending the past 23 years with her as her business partner and husband, I have an excess of gratitude that I get to walk this planet with her. Tammie is simply the best the world can give you in another human being. I love you.

My precocious, budding writer and activist of a child, Sedona Verrett, has inspired me in ways they can't imagine. As a prolific writer even at the age of 15, Sedona has introduced me to brilliant wordplay, spectacular creativity, and the tenacity of a dedicated artist. As an anti-gun-violence advocate, Sedona has the poise and advocacy skills of a seasoned activist. As I often say, I'm the opening act or hype man to Sedona, who will eclipse anything I achieve in my career. To the future household name in Hollywood, Washington, and/or Brussels, I love you.

I want to also thank my siblings, Lester McKee, Jeannine Verrett, and Stan Verrett, as well as my mother, Dr. Joyce Verrett, and my late father, Wilbert Verrett, for being such incredible role models for excellence and achievement. I love you.

I've been blessed by some amazing teachers and professors in my life. You are lucky if you get one teacher who changes your life. I had Leonard Augustine, Joseph McCormick, Dale Sinos, Charles Ogletree, David Wilkins, and quite a few more who imparted brilliance into my young and developing mind. Thank you for your dedication and mentorship.

I'd like to thank Bill Falloon at Wiley for believing in this book from the very moment he finished reading the executive summary. I've learned so much from the team at Wiley and I'm grateful for our partnership.

I'd like to thank my writing partner, Peter Birkeland, in as big of a way as possible. When I began thinking about this project, I envisioned writing this alone. When someone suggested a writing partner, I envisioned a Black woman and me talking about DEI, using shorthand about these sometimes complex topics, reminiscing about shared social and career experiences as Black professionals, and finishing each other's sentences as we quickly completed chapter after chapter. That's just how your unconscious mind works. I don't know anyone, however, who could have helped me complete this project as well as Pete, a middle-aged white writer and former professor, CEO, and board chair. I realized after our fourth conversation as Pete and I wrestled with a very nuanced DEI topic, that he was the reader I was trying to influence. Earlier in his career Pete had been the executive and hiring manager I needed to convert to a DEI champion. He was the perfect sparring partner for this topic and I'm grateful for the hard work he put into making *The Pomegranate Principle* come to life.

I'd like to thank the staff at Starbucks in Potomac and Bethesda, Maryland; the good people at Busboys and Poets in Washington, DC; and my new friends at Luar da Barra and Groupeto Bike Café in Lisbon, Portugal, for accommodating me over the many collective cups of coffee, glasses of wine, and wonderful meals I enjoyed while I typed away at your warm and welcoming establishments. And to the late Miles Davis, Nina Simone, Ahmad Jamal, and bands like Khruangbin and Cortex, thank you for producing and performing the wonderful music that served as the background soundtrack to this writing process.

Finally, I'd like to thank God for the blessing of being able to write this book. I'm a Christian and my views on diversity, equity, and inclusion are wonderfully consistent with my faith. I have been blessed by my family, friends, mentors, and work colleagues with great advice and support, but my career truly shifted when I changed the way I prayed. Instead of praying for a specific outcome like a new job, or promotion, or raise, I started praying this way: "God send me where you need me to be, and I promise I will show up prepared to deliver excellence and expertise to whoever needs it at the time."

In the spirit of that prayer, I hope this book gets into the hands of leaders who want to improve their diversity, equity, and inclusion strategies in recruiting, and that they find it to be excellent expertise they can use every day.

ABOUT
THE AUTHORS

Rory E. Verrett is the founder and managing partner of Protégé Search, the leading global executive search firm focused on diverse talent. Protégé Search recruits board members, C-suite leaders, and management-level talent for consumer, tech, media, sports, and financial services companies, and mission-based organizations such as think tanks, foundations, universities, and trade associations.

Rory is a graduate of Harvard Law School and Howard University. He was previously a leader in the diversity practices of two global executive search firms, the first-ever head of talent management at the National Football League, and the co-head of the diversity strategy practice at The Raben Group.

Rory has shared his innovative insights on diversity and inclusion with *Fortune* and *Forbes* magazines, the *New York Times*, and as a moderator and speaker at Harvard University, and Stanford, Duke, and Wharton business schools.

A global expert on DEI and inclusive recruiting, Rory has worked and lectured on diversity initiatives in Australia, Africa, and Europe. Rory has also testified before the U.S. Congress as a national expert on diversity and inclusion in corporate America. He is the host of the award-winning Protégé Podcast, a career advice show focused on the career journeys of diverse professionals and leaders. Rory is a former trustee of Howard University, the past president of the Harvard Law Black Alumni Association, an independent board member of Bolster, and a member of Alpha Phi Alpha Fraternity, Incorporated.

Peter M. Birkeland is a sociologist, author, and writer who collaborates with people to help them turn their ideas into books. More about his work can be found at www.peterbirkeland.com.

INTRODUCTION:
Growing Up as a Pomegranate

So that you understand where I am coming from, it is important for you to know where I came from. After all, this is a book about recruiting diverse professionals and leaders to your organization, and how I came to propose this framework is rooted in both my career experiences as a Black man, as well as my personal background.

My childhood was steeped in Black excellence. I grew up in New Orleans, Louisiana, in the 1970s and 1980s in a blue-collar neighborhood in New Orleans East. My parents, who intentionally moved to this all-Black neighborhood to be role models in the community, were doting, loving, stern, and fun. My father, who had to leave middle school to support his mother during the Depression, was a World War II veteran, cement mason, and president of his local union. He was also the president of our church, his civic club, and the founder of a Black voter education initiative. My mother was a brilliant student, professor, and university administrator. She was valedictorian of her high school class in New Orleans, her college class at Dillard University, and her master's degree class at NYU. She graduated with a PhD in biology from Tulane University and served as professor, dean, and provost at three Historically Black Colleges and Universities (HBCUs) and a state university. She was awarded two Fulbright scholarships. I've come across a lot of smart people in my life, but my mother, Dr. Joyce Verrett, is the most brilliant person I've ever met.

I was the youngest of four children, and my siblings set a very high bar for academic achievement. My oldest brother, Lester, entered college after his junior year in high school. My sister, Jeannine, attended a gifted and talented high school, won the state competition in French twice, studied in France at the Sorbonne her junior year, and graduated from college in three-and-a-half years. My brother Stan was senior class president in high school, a National Merit Scholar, and the co-anchor of Howard University's television station. Each of them attended college on scholarship. They are now a president of a foundation, a high school French teacher, and a sportscaster on ESPN. Needless to say, my parents' expectations were sky-high when I entered high school.

I enjoyed every single minute of my high school experience. I attended an all-Black, all-boys Catholic high school, St. Augustine. St. Augustine was founded in 1951 in New Orleans by the Josephite Fathers and Brothers for the education of Black male Catholic students, although it was open to students from any race who could pass the admissions test. The priests and lay teachers called you "mister" and used your last name. Being called "Mr. Verrett" for any reason—a correct answer, talking in class, arriving late—had a magical quality to it for us teenage Black boys. As an adult, I realized the additional power of attending an all-Black, all-boys school: it helped frame academic achievement in the archetype of Black men. Every nerd, every science geek, every future politician I would meet, compete against, and become friends with had brown skin and wavy or kinky hair. For the five years I attended St. Aug and long thereafter, I unconsciously associated excellence with being Black and male.

St. Aug had an illustrious history, and we were encouraged as Purple Knights (our school mascot) to uphold that rich legacy. Our basketball and football teams had integrated the segregated state athletic association, our marching band integrated Mardi Gras, and our alumni served in prominent roles in politics and business in the city, state, and around the country. The white and Black priests and lay faculty pounded into our impressionable heads the fact that much was expected of us, and that we were equal to the challenge.

I found my groove in my sophomore year of high school when I joined the speech and debate team. I received a second place trophy in my first tournament and was hooked on National Forensic League competitions. I won the state championship in drama and placed fourth in the nation in duo reading of literature in my junior year and won the state championship in oratory and the city championships in oratory, duo reading, and prose-poetry reading my senior year. I was captain of the team my senior year and St. Aug came in second as a team in the state championships. We won first place as a team in 11 of 13 city and state tournaments. If the state championships weren't so heavily weighted in favor of debate, our team would have won the state championship, as we dominated the speech/acting events. Despite the fact that I was student body president, band announcer, and ranked seventh in my class, I still had time to devote 20 hours or more per week to preparing for and competing in speech and debate tournaments. I loved every minute of competing in speech, and after winning 85 trophies, I think it loved me a little bit, too.

I attended Howard University, the nation's preeminent HBCU, for college. At Howard, I basked in Black academic excellence a second time, but this time accompanied by Black women students. Like St. Aug, Howard bestowed upon its students an inspirational, but heavy burden: we were the inheritors of courageous change agents who helped secure freedom and equality for Black Americans. The academic ghosts of Toni Morrison,

Thurgood Marshall, Andrew Young, David Dinkins, and hundreds of others loomed over our matriculation like brilliant, tough-love parents hoping their children understood the high price of mediocrity. I excelled within this nurturing environment, graduating *magna cum laude* and *Phi Beta Kappa*, serving as the elected student trustee on Howard's board, and winning a Truman Scholarship from my home state of Louisiana.

I then attended Harvard Law School immediately after graduating from Howard. Harvard Law was in turmoil in the early 1990s: Derrick Bell, the first Black tenured professor at the law school, took a leave of absence and threatened to not return until Harvard appointed a woman of color to the faculty. Most Black students supported Bell and protested on his behalf about the lack of faculty diversity. When I entered the law school in the fall of 1992, the Black third-year students and a couple of Black professors, Charles Ogletree and David Wilkins, had set up a unique orientation for incoming Black students. Harvard Law was my first time attending a primarily white institution (PWI), and I didn't know what to expect regarding my white classmates, living in Cambridge, or the cold weather in New England.

I thrived at Harvard as well. I did respectably academically but found my groove again in extracurricular activities. I was elected one of the four class marshals for my class, helped edit the *Harvard Journal on Legislation,* and served as a student attorney at the Harvard Legal Aid Bureau. I was also a student activist with the Coalition for Civil Rights, a campus group that advocated for greater faculty diversity. Although the law school was somewhat balkanized socially, I found it easy to hang out with my classmates regardless of their background. I moved seamlessly among white, Black, Hispanic/Latine, and Asian American circles, but the Black Law Students Association (BLSA) was my social base. The Black students at the law school encouraged each other, hosted soul food parties, and shared information about which law firms had the best track record on diversity.

My experiences at St. Aug, Howard, and Harvard Law were steeped in Black excellence. These academic moments profoundly informed my perspective as an executive recruiter and diversity consultant. Simply put, until I was 22 years old, much of the brilliance, genius, and incredible talent I experienced in my life had a Black face to it. Of course, I knew from competing in speech and debate, traveling around the country and Europe as a teenager, and my time in college and law school that there were accomplished people from many different racial backgrounds. But I understood and felt most intimately the excellence of Black people.

I never once considered Black to be a proxy or code word for subpar, less than, inferior, or anything other than excellence. Growing up in a blue-collar Black neighborhood that slowly devolved into a haven for drug use and crime, I saw teenage pregnancy, criminal behavior, and family dysfunction in Black faces as well. The mainstream media also helped promote a narrative of Black dysfunction. But growing up in my family, my education at St. Aug, Howard, and Harvard Law, and being surrounded by so much Black excellence so early in my life would profoundly shape my perspective on what excellence looked like.

My career has also furthered my exposure to Black excellence, but I won't belabor every move I've made in my career here, as I will intersperse my experiences throughout the book. I began my career as an attorney at a big law firm, but quickly realized I didn't like big law firms nor the practice of law. I joined the staff of my local congressman, William Jefferson, whom I'd interned with between college and law school. I worked briefly at Entergy, a utility company in Louisiana, as a lobbyist. I then ran for political office twice in Louisiana, losing a state house race, but winning a seat on the Democratic State Committee from the same district. I started diversiplex.com, an internet company, with some college friends and managed that company for five years. I then entered the executive search industry on a fluke. I was a candidate for a vice president of governmental affairs role and the recruiting firm turned the tables and began recruiting me to work for the firm.

I worked at two of the big executive search firms, Russell Reynolds Associates and Spencer Stuart, over a period of six years. While at Spencer Stuart, I worked on two assignments for the National Football League, and the NFL eventually hired me to be the first-ever head of talent management at the league office in New York. In that role, I managed executive recruiting; executive education for the top executives at the 32 clubs; an internal leadership academy for high potential, mid-career executives; and succession planning for senior management. I worked at the NFL for three years before joining the Raben Group, a diversity and public affairs firm in Washington, DC. While at the Raben Group, I launched an online show on careers, Protégé Podcast. That show garnered the attention of a few corporations interested in me helping them with executive coaching and recruiting, something the Raben Group did not offer. In 2016, I launched Protégé Search, an executive recruiting and leadership advisory firm focused on diverse talent.

That's my career in a nutshell. In essence, the first half of my life was marinated in Black excellence, and the second half has been trying to help companies, organizations, and professionals understand that excellence comes in Black and many other shades and forms.

WHO THIS BOOK IS FOR

Let me be blunt: I didn't write this book to convince you that diversity matters. If you're on the fence about diversity, equity, and inclusion (DEI), if you don't see a business case for innovation, if you don't want to create a foothold in new markets, if you're not interested in growing your organization, if you don't want to thrive during unpredictable times, then this book won't convince you—and it's not written for you. There are dozens of books written on diversity that can help your company establish a diversity strategy, manage employee resource groups, or deal with a racism crisis. Roosevelt Thomas wrote a classic book on diversity over 30 years ago, *Beyond Race and Gender*, and David Thomas, president of Morehouse College, also wrote a seminal work on the experiences of Blacks in corporate America, *Breaking Through.*

This book is about how to successfully recruit diverse talent. It's the book I wish I had when I was starting my career as a diversity and inclusion professional 25 years ago. It's meant to help your company or organization incorporate these principles into your recruiting efforts, whether you have 500+ talent acquisition professionals spread across five continents, or you are a startup founder trying to incorporate diversity as a first principle in your company's culture.

It's important to get diversity recruiting right because recruiting diverse talent is the linchpin of creating more DEI in your organization. And the reason you want to create more DEI in your organization ought to be clear: by tapping into the productivity and the innovation and creativity of different generations, of different ethnic groups, of different genders, of different learning styles, of people who come into the organization who provide their life experience and professional experience, you will reap tremendous rewards. Because all of these elements coalesce to create amazing breakthrough concepts, new products, new services, and access to new markets. This book is for those people who are trying to do it, but find themselves stuck, faltering, or unable to sustain momentum.

This book is primarily a handbook for hiring managers at companies, startups, professional services firms, nonprofits, and universities. It's also, however, a guide for everyone in the organization. Executive leaders, inclusive of, but not limited to, the CEO, the chief diversity officer, and the chief human resources officer are responsible for establishing the overarching

DEI vision, which includes diversity recruiting. Hiring managers are largely on the front lines of executing the diversity recruiting strategy as they build out their teams. And professionals at all levels are the employees existing in the culture of the organization, whether it's diverse, inclusive, equitable, or not. As such, rank-and-file employees play an important role in advocating, monitoring, and promoting the success of DEI strategies, including diversity recruiting.

I am a big believer in simplicity, and I have organized the book into three sections. Part I introduces the Pomegranate Principle as a recruiting strategy and details the nature of the twenty-first-century talent pool and the structural challenges in the market that companies face in recruiting diverse talent. Part II is about the techniques and processes that companies should *stop* doing because, while perhaps well-intentioned, they may serve to thwart the successful recruitment of diverse talent. Part III is a deep dive into the larger set of Pomegranate Principles, the solutions that can be implemented in your organization that will help you attract and retain diverse talent. I have found that a lot of companies just make this more complicated than it is. There are a few things that companies have to get right, and then there's a lot of whitespace to add the particular dimensions you need for your company to succeed in this area. In this book I break down best practices of diversity recruitment and provide simple guidelines that any organization can follow.

This book, and the search firm I started, are for hiring managers who have already decided they want to recruit and retain diverse talent. You already have the reasons why you want more diversity and now you need to make your efforts work. You may have tried a particular diversity initiative and it didn't work out, and you're wondering what you can do to make it better. I wrote this book for those of you who want to succeed at diversity recruiting and who want to do it at an expert level and who want a proven list of best practices to implement.

PROTÉGÉ SEARCH: Our Mission and Methodology as a Diversity Recruiting Firm

I am proud to be the founder of Protégé Search, an executive recruiting firm focused on diverse talent. When I say diverse talent, I really consider that to be shorthand for managing an inclusive leadership hiring process for corporations, startups, trade associations, and nonprofit organizations. An inclusive leadership hiring process means sourcing broadly for the absolute best talent for a leadership position at an organization. Inclusive leadership hiring means having professionals from a wide diversity of backgrounds on the candidate slate, including leaders with Hispanic/Latine, Caucasian, Black, Asian American, and Indigenous backgrounds. It means candidates who are veterans, who are neurodivergent, and who are LGBTQ. We don't submit slates of candidates who are all Black because it would be narrowminded and factually incorrect to support the belief that only Black people are the best qualified to lead a function or business unit. We don't submit slates of candidates who are all Caucasian for the same reason. The data and the talent market do not support such a narrow view of excellence.

We tell our prospective clients that we don't have some secret database of brilliant and accomplished leaders of color that other search firms don't have. With online databases like LinkedIn, which has 900 million profiles of professionals from 200 countries, ZoomInfo, which has 235 million profiles, and the dozens of other online candidate databases, candidate profiles are widely available to anyone with a computer and a paid account with these services.

Why then do companies, nonprofits, and big search firms still struggle to deliver diverse candidates on their slates? There are many factors to this failure that we will explore in detail in the book. I think the main reason big search firms fail is the commercial churn at the core of their business model. Executive recruiters at the large, global executive search firms are paid to bring in business, first and foremost, and then to execute as many searches as possible. Unless a client really demands it, big search firms typically are going to provide token effort to recruit a truly diverse slate because an inclusive slate, like a great pot of Creole gumbo, takes time to make. There's simply no real incentive to do that at the big, global executive search firms. The reason organizations don't create diverse slates via their internal recruiting teams is also somewhat related to the time it takes to curate a diverse slate, but it's more, I think, about in-house expertise regarding inclusive hiring methodologies.

That is the purpose of this book: to share the techniques we employ at Protégé Search on behalf of our clients, as well as the strategies that we've observed at companies and organizations that are excellent at diversity recruiting. This book is written for the hiring managers at companies, startups, trade associations, and nonprofits that have the intention to do diversity recruiting well, but who might benefit from applying some best practices to their current efforts.

Our firm's ethos as a diversity recruiting firm is categorically different from what clients get from the big executive search firms and from what most boutique firms offer. As I noted, we don't have some secret cache of diverse leadership profiles. As the president of the Harvard Law Black Alumni Association, a member of Alpha Phi Alpha Fraternity, Incorporated, a former trustee of Howard University, and an extrovert, I will admit that I'm very well-networked within professional communities of color. The nine consultants at our firm are also well-networked. But that alone is not what adds value to our clients. We have a proven methodology that works over and over again to help the world's most innovative companies and the most impactful organizations execute an inclusive leadership hiring process for C-suite leaders and their direct reports, the usual roles we recruit for our clients. Our clients at Protégé Search include well-known companies and organizations, such as The New York Times Company, the Seattle Mariners, the San Francisco Giants, Peloton, Pinterest, PayPal, Ben & Jerry's, Tapestry, Freddie Mac, the U.S. House of Representatives, the American Medical Association, New America, Legal Services Corporation, and the National Society of Black Engineers. Our clients also include smaller, perhaps lesser-known companies and organizations, including Mercury Fund, Twilio, ZenDesk, fhi 360, Inatai Foundation, Dillard University, and the New Orleans Culinary and Hospitality Institute (NOCHI).

One of my favorite client projects was the search for the CEO of Paisley Park, Prince's concert venue, recording studio, and home. I spent a recent summer leading that search along with leading the search for the executive director of NOCHI. That meant toggling my time between Chanhassen, Minnesota, and my hometown of New Orleans, Louisiana. Executive search is hard on a good day, very difficult on most days, but discussing the search with Prince's bandmates and family one week in Minneapolis, and then dining out with restaurant royalty in New Orleans to understand emerging trends in the culinary arts scene in Louisiana made for an unforgettable summer.

Food and music are not only two of my favorite things to indulge in, but they're also two subjects I always use to make metaphors about recruiting and careers. As an executive coach, I tell candidates to think about the greatest hits in their careers as part of an assessment I conduct. I ask them to imagine that they are Prince: What's their "Purple Rain," "Raspberry Beret," "1999," "Pop Life," and "Kiss" as career achievements? As a recruiter, I tell our prospective clients that we don't look at other search firms for inspiration. We look to food and wine entrepreneurs, the restaurateurs and winemakers of the world. The best restaurants in the world aren't the chain varieties, they are almost always single destinations for a spectacular culinary experience. Their growth is not modeled after Morton's Steakhouse, which strives for consistency across its many locations. Instead, their growth is about providing an incredible experience for each customer, becoming more creative and innovative year by year, but never losing sight of what makes them unique in the market. The same is true with the world's most heralded winemakers, whose goal is to create an excellent vintage year after year, carefully melding new process innovations with their existing grape varietals and unique terroir.

In that tradition of great restaurants and vineyards, I want Protégé Search to be the Dooky Chase of executive recruiting. Dooky Chase is an 80-year-old Creole restaurant in New Orleans. Until her passing in 2019 (the year I did the NOCHI executive director search), Leah Chase still came to the restaurant every day, stirring the pot of her legendary gumbo. She inspired generations to take up the mantle of preserving this great culinary tradition of Creole cooking. Dooky Chase has served as a place where the influential gathered and enjoyed spectacular service. Icons such as Martin Luther King, Jr., President Barack Obama, James Baldwin, Michelle Obama, Beyoncé, Duke Ellington, Thurgood Marshall, and Ray Charles have all dined at Dooky Chase. It is also the place that locals in New Orleans go to for the best Creole cooking in town. It's not Burger King and it's not Morton's Steakhouse, both of whom dwarf Dooky Chase in terms of revenue. Dooky Chase is also not the well-intentioned server in the food court in many malls in America asking you to sample "Bourbon Chicken," a quick-serve imitation of Creole food. Somewhere between the big, impersonal chain with a couple of Creole dishes on the menu and the hastily prepared imitation in the food court is the sacred space that Dooky Chase occupies in the world of Creole cooking. That's my hope for Protégé Search: that we provide an excellently curated and deeply expert experience for our clients, and that we provide an incredibly valuable and authentic service to the world's most influential leaders.

Several years ago, I interviewed to be the chief diversity officer at a major technology company in California. As I was speaking with the CEO, he asked me, "What's the one thing you want to tell me? What's the one thing you want me to know?" And I told him that "DEI is not going to be successful unless you, as CEO, are perpetually uncomfortable about this." That's a measuring stick because at the end of the day, DEI is disruptive. It's like any other change management initiative: you will have early adopters, late adopters, and those who silently or overtly oppose the initiative. This particular CEO was also an amateur bodybuilder, so I shared with him the following analogy. How does your trainer approach you when you go to the gym? Are they kind to you? Are they supportive? They might be, but they're trying to get you to change your behavior, and that will probably make you uncomfortable. The same is true when you go see a doctor. They may be kind and empathetic, but at the end of the day, it's tough love. And that is what creating more diversity is—it's trying to change the institutional behaviors of an enterprise to be much more aligned with equity, anti-racism, justice, and fairness. It's not that it's a never-ending effort, it's not that you're going to be uncomfortable every day at work until your career ends, but it is a long-term strategy. As Martin Luther King, Jr, said, "Let us realize the arc of the moral universe is long, but it bends toward justice." The core of this book is helping people get comfortable with the things that make them uncomfortable because, when it comes to leadership and change and disruption—all these things that are bedeviling societies—diversity, demographic change, how we all live together in prosperity and harmony—that's going to provide perpetual disruption over the next few decades.

This book is for those who want to lean into that disruption and harness it for the better.

****

A word about vocabulary. The diversity, equity, and inclusion (DEI) sector is rife with a culture of precision about terminology and vocabulary. Words have real meaning, and we can unintentionally offend if we don't know the import, origin, or nuance around language as we wade into the murky waters of race, class, sexual orientation, and gender identity. Again, in the spirit of clarity and simplicity, I'm going to take license to use certain words and phrases throughout the book. I acknowledge that there is some ambiguity with using these terms and that the terminology in the DEI sector is constantly changing. I also acknowledge that others might use them differently. I have not been the type of DEI practitioner to vigilantly police words and definitions in conversations or training sessions. Yes, certain words do matter, but I believe we stymie understanding when we police the ever-evolving language in this sector too aggressively and punitively. Most people, I have found, are well-intentioned, but perhaps undereducated about words and terms in the DEI space. I hope my good intentions in this book overcome any offense in using certain terms in certain ways.

For purposes of this book, I'm going to use the phrase *diverse talent* to mean talent inclusive of what has been termed underrepresented minorities (URM) or BIPOC (Black, Indigenous, and people of color) talent. I recognize that *diverse talent* technically includes everyone, including Caucasian professionals, but I'm going to bet on the reader understanding the context of the term in different scenarios. I will also use the terms *candidates of color* and *professionals of color* as proxies for the term *diverse talent*. For instance, a hiring manager can be looking to source diverse talent—candidates of color—for a role and, in that case, it means looking for URM talent. That same executive also might feel proud when the slate of candidates for a particular role, which includes URM and Caucasian candidates, is diverse and representative of the broader consumer market the company serves. In this scenario, *diverse talent* can have two meanings depending on its usage. I have had very spirited conversations with fellow DEI practitioners about using the term *diverse talent* in these ways. Some agree with my model, others disagree. No one violently disagrees. I am in no way suggesting that my framework is the only one to use, but this book is about convincing you, a hiring manager, to adopt certain principles and techniques in diversity recruiting, and I'm hoping the utility of the terminology I use helps achieve that outcome.

I hesitate to use *URM* as the primary term in the book because I think URM is contextual for whether, in fact, that talent is underrepresented in a particular market. Are Latinos URMs in California? Are Black professionals URMs in the Northeast? And I think *BIPOC* is not yet understood or embraced by large swaths of the market. In many cases, I also use the word *Black* versus *African American*, as Black covers a broader set of people than African American (it can include, for instance, Black people from the Caribbean or South America or Fiji or other countries who are brown skinned but who do not have direct ties to Africa and don't consider themselves of African descent).

I'm going to use the words *Hispanic/Latine* to capture the collective group of very diverse people that have been described as Latino, Latina and Hispanic because I believe these are the most inclusive and gender-neutral terms in current usage. There is currently broad debate and disagreement in the Hispanic/Latine community about the use of the term *Latinx* as an overarching term. I don't believe that any current terms completely and accurately capture the complexity and comprehensiveness of people who are from (or whose families are from) Spanish-speaking countries and Latin America. My sense is there would be some debate about any term that might be used. Again, I hope no one takes offense on the usage of these terms.

Lastly, I capitalize the word *Black* and not the word *white* throughout the book. There are reasonable arguments for capitalizing both and there is vigorous debate within the DEI community on this issue. I believe *Black* should be capitalized because it signifies a group of people associated with a particular set of cultural values and traditions. I do not capitalize *white* because I do not believe white signifies a group of people with the same kinds of cultural bonds. Capitalizing *Black* and not capitalizing *white* does not mean I am anti-white. The distinction acknowledges the difference between a more cohesive racial group—Black people—than one that is not as similarly cohesive—white people—who tend to identify more by nationality than race.

Language matters and, within the DEI space, there is constant evolution about terms. I have sought counsel from leaders from a variety of backgrounds to make sure I am inclusive and nonoffensive. When in doubt, I have deferred to what leaders of civil rights organizations in these communities have expressed as their preferred terms, rather than what is in popular usage at the moment within society or the DEI practitioner space. I hope that my use of these terms in the book does not offend anyone. That is emphatically the opposite of what I intended.

PART I

THE STRUCTURE OF THE TALENT MARKET

FINDING POMEGRANATES

The Pomegranate Principle is a framework about how and why we select things and how we can overcome our biases in these selections to experience tremendous benefit and value. When you go into a supermarket, do you ever notice how fruits are arranged? Typically, you see the apples first.

1

Red and shiny, available in different varieties, apples greet you with their all-American essence, proudly welcoming you to the land of produce. You probably notice the citrus fruits next. Organized neatly in their own prime real estate, oranges and their citrus cousins are bold, beautiful, and reflect the sunshine of their native lands. You probably also see bananas, grapes, and maybe cherries, mangoes, and pears.

But do you ever notice the pomegranates? Almost always, pomegranates are located near other exotic fruit, typically sharing aisle space with kiwi, star fruit, and dragon fruit. If you are not looking for pomegranates, you probably won't find them. These incredibly powerful "superfruits" might escape your attention unless you have purchased them before and know exactly where to find them. And if you have ever had a pomegranate, well, you know how wonderful and beneficial they can be.

The more important question is: Why do we overlook this powerful fruit? I have a theory about this. I think it is because fruits like apples and oranges are beneficial and valuable to us and, most of all, they are *safe*. You give your teacher an apple to curry favor. The well-known advice to eat more fruits and vegetables emphasizes "an apple a day keeps the doctor away." What is more American than *apple* pie?

Given the apple's cultural dominance, the pomegranate barely stands a chance of being selected by the casual grocery shopper. It takes a fair amount of purposefulness and familiarity to go find the pomegranates, buy them, and consume them. But if you have ever had a pomegranate, you know how rich they are in antioxidants, how versatile they are in various recipes, and how simply enjoyable they are. These superfruits, though, are different from apples and oranges. If you measure them by how apples and oranges look, pomegranates can look dented, possibly rotten, or simply irregular. Pomegranates are different *and* they are powerfully valuable additions to your diet.

I think the talent market in the United States is set up like the produce section in most supermarkets. White men are the apples. White women are the citrus fruits. Black, Hispanic/Latine, Indigenous, and some Asian American professionals are the pomegranates, kiwi, dragon fruit, and star fruit. We're in the market, but we are not showcased as prominently as the apples or, in many cases, like the oranges. We don't look like apples and oranges. We are not experienced like apples and oranges. And it was a very different journey for many of us to show up in that market versus the apples and oranges.

The larger point is this: if you went to the supermarket to find the most beneficial and nutritious fruits, regardless of your preconceived notions, it is likely you would wind up with a different allocation of fruit than what you typically purchase. There would be a few more pomegranates and kiwis, and perhaps not as many apples and oranges. We do not select our fruits this way because the produce section is primarily set up to showcase apples and oranges. Why? One reason is because the agricultural associations supporting the apple and orange industries are powerful and leverage their power in Congress and in state legislatures. It is not an accident that you can always find apples and oranges in great supply. These fruits have lobbyists and organizations supporting their viability and their ubiquity. As a result, when most of us think about fruit, apples and oranges come to mind. With the ubiquitous marketing, cultural primacy, and safety of selecting apples and oranges among consumers, it is no wonder we select them over and over again.

The central thrust of the Pomegranate Principle is this: the talent market is set up like the supermarket produce section, and if you are not purposeful and intentional about your selections, you are bound to make the same decisions over and over again. The Pomegranate Principle offers a metaphor for how we select nontraditional talent in companies and organizations. Nontraditional talent includes professionals and executives from diverse backgrounds, including candidates from under-represented minority groups such as Black, Hispanic/Latine, Indigenous, and Southeast Asian communities. Understanding how our bias impacts our hiring decisions is the first step, among many, to successfully recruiting and retaining diverse talent.

To be clear, the talent market is not set up for you to easily find diverse talent in the same way the produce section is not set up for you to easily find pomegranates. That does not mean that there is an absence of diversity in the market. Such is rarely the case. Are there fewer candidates of color available for certain positions in some cases? Certainly. But in 25 years in the DEI industry, I have never failed to present qualified diverse candidates on a client recruiting project.

WHAT YOU ARE UP AGAINST IN YOUR DIVERSITY RECRUITING EFFORTS

Just like the produce section does not make it easy for you to find pomegranates, the U.S. talent market does not make it easy for you to recruit diverse talent. There are some headwinds you inevitably will encounter that will make your efforts challenging at times. Acknowledging these market forces can provide you with a practical, realistic, and long-term strategy to diversify your organization. Let's first identify what you are up against so you can you meet the actual challenges confronting your organization in recruiting diverse talent.

CHAPTER ONE

THE LABOR MARKET

Labor markets are always dynamic, always changing, but usually there are submarkets that operate independently from the economy as a whole. In one part of the country, there may be a huge demand for teachers, for example, but an oversupply of engineers; in other parts of the country, there may be demand for retail workers while there is an oversupply of marketers. And, of course, labor markets differ by sector, and we see today that 94% of retailers are dealing with job vacancy issues. Rarely in the history of the United States do we find what is happening now with the Great Resignation (see Figure 1.1). Today, regardless of industry, job, or location, the thought bubble over the heads of many professionals is something like this: "I am quitting my job because of the [toxicity/banality/purposelessness] of the culture where I work." There have always been people who quit their jobs, but it has never happened before at this scale. In 2021, 48 million people quit their jobs. The year 2021 wasn't a unique year because in 2022 we are still averaging above 4 million people quitting their job *every month*.[1] And this is not just a U.S. economy issue; over 40% of the global workforce is thinking of quitting their jobs. The idea of a job shortage, or the term "Great Resignation," were not even topics people cared about until 2021.

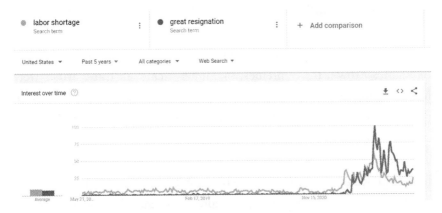

Figure 1.1 Google search trends "Job Shortage" and "Great Resignation."

Now, the idea that people would choose to not work is commonplace, and if you think you have all the leverage as a hiring manager, as a boss, you are tragically wrong. It does not mean that you have to capitulate to every demand from every worker and it does not mean that you have to double the salaries of everyone, but it does mean that you have to meet people where they are and understand the cultural and generational influences impacting people's engagement. You will have to navigate through evolving cultural expectations about work to get the best productivity and leadership value out of your staff. So, the first headwind you face as an organization, the first structural issue impacting your ability to recruit professionals and leaders of color is the Great Resignation. It is a phenomenon impacting all professionals, regardless of race or gender, as Figure 1.1 shows.

THE LURE OF ENTREPRENEURSHIP

A second major factor impacting your organization's ability to recruit and retain diverse talent is the incredible pull of entrepreneurship. There has been explosive growth of celebrity entrepreneurs, and today's celebrity is vastly different than celebrities in the past, especially for entertainers. Forty or fifty years ago, if you look at entertainers from the 1960s and 1970s, like James Brown, the Supremes, or Lionel Richie, all those artists were just celebrities. They sold their music and made their money. But now, in the 2000s, we have artists and entrepreneurs like Rihanna, who is a music star but also has a cosmetics line, or Jay-Z, who has a record label, a talent agency, a publishing house, a clothing line, and a nonprofit associated with his brand. Rihanna and Jay-Z have redefined what it means to be a celebrity because they are celebrities, entrepreneurs, and business moguls and they have built empires that have made them billionaires.

But even though they are powerful (or because of their power) they still wear hats and hoodies and athletic shoes. That is powerful signaling in a status-conscious culture like America. What this also says to people is, "Wow, there is a way for me to be successful in America and not have to spend so much time trying to make white people feel comfortable." So, people of color see that, and they think there is more to life than working for a company—I can start my own business. I am inspired to do my own thing. And it is not just the kid in the housing project who is thinking that way; it is also the Harvard or Stanford Business School graduate who is working at Goldman Sachs or McKinsey & Company. While a lot of people do not have the sort of psychological makeup to actually become an entrepreneur, or they may not have the cushion financially since they have real-world income needs and can't take that kind of financial risk, it is a thought that they have—it is in the back of everyone's mind.

For people of color, we have seen vast changes in entrepreneurship that bear out this new mentality: entrepreneurship among Black women soared over the past decade to 322% with over $51 billion in revenue, and Latino-owned businesses account for 34% of startups.[2] I once approached a Black male partner at McKinsey about a very senior leadership opportunity. As I was easing into my pitch about the role and how it seemed like a logical next step for him in his career, he kept pulling the conversation back to my firm, Protégé Search. I kept thinking that he was just being gracious and complimentary about our success. But he was serious. He declined the corporate role, a front office leadership position at a professional sports franchise, because his next step—his ultimate goal—was to run his own company.

The pull of entrepreneurship with diverse talent is not a new phenomenon but its dimensions are vastly different now. Black communities have always bestowed on the owners of funeral homes, insurance companies, and dentist, doctor, and lawyer offices premium social status. Immigrant communities have historically had grocery stores, restaurants, and other services businesses in their communities as well. These businesses provided their owners with not only wealth-building platforms for their families, but they also provided a source of charitable giving in communities of color. They provided the first internships in these communities. I have noted jokingly that of all of the types of middle-class Black Americans, these millionaire-next-door types have been the ones sponsoring the Black Little League team, providing internships for Black teenagers and college students, and, if you are lucky to have a self-made entrepreneur in your family, they have probably paid for the funeral costs for an elderly relative or two.

So, what is different about the Black and brown entrepreneurs of today versus 30 or 40 years ago?

There are three important differences. The first is their ubiquity. Nearly every time a young student or professional of color hums along to a Rihanna or Beyoncé or Future song, they almost always hum along to a lyric about that artist's entrepreneurial ventures. In a genius stroke of promotion, this generation's hip-hop and R&B artists are pushing their champagne, cosmetics, and clothing lines within their songs. As hip-hop entrepreneurial pioneer Sean "Puff Daddy" Combs noted, the goal is to have their consumers listen to their music, use their cologne, wear their clothes, and go to their restaurants and nightclubs. It is a completely integrated brand of products and services first introduced via the artist's music.

The second difference is the youth of these entrepreneurs. It can be hard to make a career shift to emulate Aunt Camille's hair salon if she is 50 years old and you are a 19-year-old sophomore at college. You might be staring at 20 dog years of getting your business up and running, establishing its brand, and servicing customers. On the other hand, young students and professionals are watching artists like Rihanna build massive wealth in an astonishingly short period of time. According to *Forbes*, Rihanna is now worth $1.7 billion. Much of that wealth does not come from her music career but comes from her business ventures. She is a 50% owner of Fenty Beauty, which provides $1.4 billion of her wealth. The rest of her wealth largely comes from her lingerie company, Savage x Fenty, which is worth an estimated $270 million. These are ventures that Rihanna started in 2017. She is now the second richest Black woman in America (next to Oprah, whose rise to billionaire status took 20 years to Rihanna's 15). Rihanna, Sean Combs, Serena Williams, LeBron James, Steph Curry, and dozens of other musical artists and professional athletes are achieving mogul status *young*. That makes waiting five years for a promotion in corporate America sound like an eternity. And Rihanna's entrepreneurial rise is telegraphed through her music, her social media posts, and other digital and traditional media. If you are a Black professional at a corporate workplace and you are singing Rihanna's song "Work," there is a good chance you are dreaming of having work like *hers*, and not the project you are managing for your boss at your employer.

The third issue that is important to recognize with the pull of celebrity entrepreneurship is that these entertainers and athletes are building businesses *on their own terms*. They are hiring professional attorneys and consultants and established business executives, but also their own family and friends as employees and partners. And they are wearing hip, casual clothes, partying, and living their best lives while they build their empires. Contrast that with the dress codes, commutes, code switching, and microaggressions that diverse talent have to endure in much of corporate America, and is it any wonder that young professionals of color opt for a life of entrepreneurship?

Put it all together and this means that your Millennial and Gen Z talent is constantly bombarded with images of rich, youthful businesspeople of color who built their wealth quickly, glamorously, and on their own cultural terms. It does not mean that it is a hopeless venture to try to recruit them, but not acknowledging this glaring reality is antithetical to any possibility of recruiting and retaining diverse talent.

The entrepreneurial mindset is something that people from all walks of life can have, but unless you are looking for it or understand some of the clues that may arise in casual conversations, you will miss it entirely. For example, on one of my Protégé podcasts I spoke with a woman who, by all outside appearances, looked like a career minded C-suite level executive at a global technology company. She had an economics degree and a law degree from Harvard, and she was senior counsel in this company. The company came to her all the time and said, "Would you like to be in our leadership development program? You are in the legal function now but we think you could broaden your skill set." And when this woman said "no," the company couldn't figure it out. Why not? Why wouldn't you want to participate in a high-profile company leadership program? In the back of her mind she is thinking, "Because I have my side hair care business and this global technology job is the means I have to build up my savings and develop my experience. The corporate job is a venture capital vehicle for me." This is not an isolated example and there are many, many people of color who are building businesses from side hustles while working in corporate America.

YOUR COMPANY'S BRAND OR REPUTATION

In addition to a talent-driven labor market, quiet quitting, and the lure of entrepreneurship, there is the issue of your company or organization's brand impacting its ability to recruit and retain diverse talent. Many organizations will pay attention to engagement surveys and exit interviews and even monitor employee feedback on sites such as Glassdoor. But few of them monitor or track feedback *specifically from employees of color about their organization.* And trust me, if you are a Fortune 1000 company, there is feedback about your company out there among communities of color.

When I was a law student at Harvard, I had to figure out where I was going to work as a summer associate after my second year of law school. Without a lawyer in my family, I was left to aggregate as much information as I could from legal industry magazines and conversations with professors and fellow law students. I soon amassed an encyclopedic knowledge of which law firms provided the quickest path to partner, which ones had very high billable hour requirements, and which ones had incidences of racism. There was one book, *The Insider's Guide to Law Firms,* that I read cover to cover a couple of times. I soon developed a reputation among my fellow law students as the go-to person for the inside scoop on which law firms were best for Black students. *The American Lawyer* ranked firms in terms of number of attorneys and annual revenue. These rankings were valuable, but they were missing important context for what the lives of professionals of color were like inside these firms.

During the summer after my second year of law school, I worked at Howrey & Simon, one of the fastest-growing firms in the country. Now a defunct law firm, Howrey in the mid-1990s was a 400-attorney litigation "boutique," and it had a reputation as an early adopter of using technology effectively in the courtroom. Howrey was ranked number four in Washington, DC, by most legal periodicals, both in terms of number of attorneys and annual revenue. Even among my Harvard Law School classmates, I felt privileged to work there.

I accepted a full-time associate role there after law school. Howrey did not have an overtly racist or toxic culture. As a Black attorney, you did not die from overt toxicity; you died from neglect. Partners routinely selected white associates over you for much-needed billable work, and few of the

Black associates had any mentors or sponsors. Even worse, toward the end of my first year there, the firm sponsored a team-building golf tournament with associates and partners playing against each other. No Black associate was invited and only one woman was invited and played in the tournament. I was working with one of the senior associates who planned the tournament and was friends with many of my white fellow first-year associates who played in the tournament. Even more, I was an avid golfer.

When a senior partner emailed the entire firm celebrating the camaraderie and fun from the golf tournament, a bunch of Black attorneys decided to meet to vent about this. "Were you invited?" "This is how white associates get ahead and we get left behind." "They say the deal happens on the golf course, but none of us were there, so . . ." were the kinds of comments we shared amid our collective frustration. I wound up writing a rebuttal to the partner's email decrying the whole event as discriminatory and indicative of the barriers that attorneys of color have in their matriculation through majority white law firms. Dozens of women, Black, Hispanic/Latine, and Asian-American attorneys applauded me calling out the firm for this exclusionary event. Some of my fellow first-year associates associated with the event were hurt and shocked by my bold reply. One even asked me why I didn't approach them individually to express my outrage. I simply reminded him that we had shared a beer at my going-away party a couple of weeks ago, and he did not feel the need to share news of the event with me then. The most interesting reaction to all of this, however, is the treatment I got by low- and mid-level Black employees. I went to the basement of the firm where the staff who handled the mailroom and copying worked to produce big copy orders. (Sidebar: No one thought it odd the optics of having the majority Black mail/copy staff in the basement, while the majority of white employees worked in sun-filled offices?) When they asked my name for the order and I got it, the manager called over the other staff, told them who I was—the author of the response about the golf tournament—and I received an impromptu, mid-afternoon standing ovation from about 30 people. In the aftermath, one legal publication picked up the controversy and wrote a short article on it with a memorable headline: "Black Associate Teed Off Over Exclusionary Golf Outing." I had given notice already that I was leaving the firm to join the staff of a member of Congress by the time of this incident, so I didn't stick around to see what came of my and our protest of the event.

What does this crazy story have to do with your company's recruiting and retention efforts with diverse talent? These kinds of stories exist in the thousands across corporate America over the past 30 years. Where are they chronicled? How do you find out about them? Where is the Glassdoor for people of color? There isn't one yet. These stories are passed around by word of mouth among people of color as they try to evaluate where they should work. I certainly shared my experience with my mentees at Harvard Law and Howard and with my coworkers in the congressman's office and with my Black golf foursome whenever the topic of workplace culture came up. And I heard my female friends' stories of being sexually harassed and passed over for promotions and asked about their hairstyles, and why they weren't married, and worse.

Put together, there is a massive amount of information about your company percolating within professional communities of color. People of color talk. We warn each other about the firms and companies to avoid, about the senior vice president who never gets reprimanded for sexual harassment, about the senior partner who has buffoonish views of Black people. At Harvard Law, 25 years ago, third-year law students would remind the incoming students to largely ignore the official rankings of law firms. There was an unofficial ranking done by Black students at top schools of which firms to look into, and which ones to avoid.

Your company and organization's reputation matters. Whether you know it or not, I am certain that professionals of color in your industry and sector know about your company or organization. Just as Black and Hispanic/Latine people talk about Atlanta and Boston in vastly different terms based on their diversity and inclusiveness, there is a very strong chance that the professionals you are seeking to recruit already have a formed opinion about what it is like to work in your organization. And in the era of social media and the power of Black Twitter, a negative story about your company can travel at warp speed to prospective professionals and executives.

FIRST-GENERATION BIG-TIME

After acknowledging the particular nuances of the twenty-first-century talent market and phenomena such as quiet quitting, the powerful pull of entrepreneurship on professionals of color, and the role your firm's reputation plays in its ability to recruit and retain diverse talent, there is still a bit more to unwrap about the market for diverse talent. From experience, I believe it is critically important to understand the unique psyche of modern-day professionals of color. In my almost 30 years of working as a mentor, executive coach, and recruiter of diverse talent and as a professional of color myself, I have learned some unique ways of thinking that define this cohort of leaders, a group I have come to understand as first-generation big-time (FGBT).

I'll tell you a quick story illustrative of an FGBT professional of color. I worked at a big company and found myself trying to navigate some fairly complex corporate politics within the executive leadership team. I sought the advice of a few mentors and friends, and I also called my mother for advice. As I noted, my mother is the smartest person I know. Period. She is a three-time valedictorian, a two-time Fulbright Scholar, a recipient of a

MacArthur Genius research fellowship, and a PhD in biology. She is also a former professor, dean, and provost. After describing the situation to her, my mother provided a quick retort: "Son, I can't help you with this." Flummoxed that the smartest person I knew was dismissing my angst because of perhaps some other pressing need, I asked her to reconsider her refusal to offer counsel. She continued: "This is above me at this point. I could help if this was standard issue politics at a university. But this is high-stakes corporate politics in the boardroom and, I'm sorry to say, this is beyond me. Good luck."

This one anecdote captures much of what I mean when I describe an FGBT professional. *A first-generation big-time professional is a highly credentialed and qualified person of color who finds themselves trying to navigate corporate politics beyond their level of experience and exposure.* They are players in the corporate tournament without the right equipment. In my case, I was not first-generation college. And I was not first generation to organizational politics. I was first generation as someone with the ambition to be a CEO of a complex corporation trying to navigate through the culture of corporate America. I was operating at a level where my functional capabilities far exceeded my understanding of how to navigate the politics of the corporate tournament. That is what it means to be first-generation big-time.

This issue came up in a meeting with Jamie Dimon, CEO of JPMorgan Chase. I met with him through a networking group of senior-level African American executives who hosted private dinners with CEOs of major corporations. Dimon asked the group of 30 of us what was the most important thing he needed to know about diversity in the workplace. I said to him, "At your level, if you have a person of color in the executive ranks who you interact with on a frequent basis, if they have arrived at that level—at one of the largest and most influential financial institutions in the world—then you have got someone who got to the top of the mountain with likely much less social infrastructure, mentoring, or support than your white colleagues." I got a blank stare. I continued: "The one thing you want to do with a person of color in the C-suite is not let that competency go dormant. And the way to do that, the way to leverage that executive of color, is to put them into business functions and business lines that are heavy with ambiguity, where the business needs out-of-the-box thinking and a leader comfortable with ambiguity."

The reason that a qualified leader of color is a likely great choice is that, in my opinion, we overindex on the leadership competency of resourcefulness. If you are JPMorganChase and you have to start a branch in Detroit, and you don't know how you are going to do that, send that leader of color. That person has already shown that they can get to the top of the mountain without the same mentorship and sponsorship as their white colleagues. They likely have a supernatural level of grit. They are not getting to the C-suite in an air-conditioned bus that rides along paved roads. They got up there by riding goats, talking to sherpas, sleeping in a cave, and then they arrive at the top and say, 'Hey, I'm here, too.' If you ask leaders of color who have become CEOs, they will tell you that grit played a much bigger role in their success than anything else. Yes, they caught some breaks like everyone else and yes, they are brilliant, but grit is always a part of the calculus. It is always a part of the formula.

Grit is a hallmark of FGBT. These professionals defy odds, surpass their upbringing and environment, and go on to make an impact in a significant way. I know this from firsthand experience. I just joined my first board of directors. In a couple of meetings, I sat next to someone who has $500 million, maybe a billion dollars, of net worth; I have never sat next to anyone with that kind of money in my life. When we do an offsite, we play at an exclusive golf course, which costs a quarter of a million dollars to join. At the driving range at this course, I am hitting balls next to a PGA Tour champion who is there with his swing coach preparing for a pro tournament in a couple of weeks. So, while I did not grow up playing on PGA Tour golf courses, I do know how to repair the divot marks and the greens when playing in a foursome. I know when you are a guest, you defer to the member, that you tip the caddies with cash, and that you wear the right clothes and shoes. There are certain protocols to follow at an exclusive golf course and it is not anything like watching a Knicks game with your buddies at your house because, to compete at the highest levels in the corporate tournament, you have to act the part even if the situation is entirely new to you. Grit, social grit in particular, is hugely important for FGBT professionals in their career.

I would put myself in the ninety-fifth percentile of understanding how to navigate within these social situations. I find myself spending a lot of time with mentees helping them understand the cultural nuances of existing in these nearly foreign environments. And it is still sometimes a challenge for me. Despite all the upper-class experiences I have had in my life, I still see them through the eyes of the little Black kid on Ray Avenue in New Orleans, with a next-door neighbor in jail for attempted murder and the biggest drug dealer in town down on the corner and everybody on welfare except for our family. No matter how comfortable I get, I look at the corporate world through that lens, and it is different. And yes, I went to Harvard Law and have spent decades in corporate America as an executive and consultant, but it was not until I was 40 that I felt truly comfortable within the affluent white culture of the average American company. I spent a decade or more learning in real time with sometimes negative consequences.

One of the defining moments for the FGBT professional is realizing that you are on your own, understanding that you have run out of cultural influencers who can help you on this journey. For me, there was not a lawyer in my immediate family. We had a distant cousin who had been a lawyer, but nobody knew what to wear at an interview, nobody knew the life of law firms. My mother could help me prepare for the Rhodes Scholarship and the Truman Scholarship application processes, but she could not help with which law firms to work at or which ones to avoid.

For many FGBT, the process of making sense of important career decisions can be haphazard and uninformed. During my second year in law school, I was internally perplexed trying to choose which firm I should work at after my second year. I was in line at the school cafeteria and a woman in my section said, "Hey, Rory, the deadline's approaching for picking your summer associate job . . . where are you going to go?" And I responded, "Well, I'm trying to decide between two firms, and I'm really stuck." After I told her the two firms, she said: "That's not even a close call—one firm is one of the fastest-growing firms in the country, and the other firm, well, you could have gone to any law school to get the job at the other firm. Take the job with the first firm." And at that moment, as a second-year law student with no other contextual framework for that decision (and as a budding FGBT attorney), that woman's testimony was gospel.

I took the job at the firm my classmate suggested. I was one of 25 first-year litigation associates, and I was largely ignored. I was subjected to daily microaggressions and that racially exclusionary golf tournament they hosted. I was miserable. I had a mentor who promised he would be available to me, but he was very busy. I was put on menial work. Looking back, the summer associate job I *did not take* might have changed my life for the better. There was a Black partner there who wanted me to be his protégé and I blew off the opportunity because this was not a high-ranked, prestigious law firm. It was not the kind of firm that the top students at Harvard, Yale, or Stanford law schools went to. The guy I dismissed was Bill Kennard, who two years later became general counsel of the Federal Communications Commission (FCC), then became chairman of the FCC, and later, Managing Director of the Carlyle Group, and finally, at the end of his career, U.S. Ambassador to the European Union.

No matter how successful my career has turned out, there is no way to spin that I made the wrong decision here. Even if I still would have quit practicing law, having a professional relationship with someone of Kennard's character and influence would have been beneficial to my career in many ways.

Hindsight, of course, often teaches us valuable lessons. This scenario is something that predictably happens to an FGBT; you have outrun your ability to frame important career decisions contextually. So, you make very dumb decisions. You select the big, prestigious law firm based on their ranking and you ignore the offer to apprentice with a powerful mentor at a less prestigious firm. You don't have anyone who can tell you that law firm rankings mean nothing about your development as a young associate. You don't have anyone to tell you that, in the first few years of any profession, a powerful mentor can supercharge your career. You are, to put it mildly, professionally clueless. You are FGBT through and through.

And if being oblivious to the basic fundamentals of smart career decision-making is not enough to stymie your development, there are the cultural cues you can miss as an FGBT. When I began at Harvard Law School I started seeing, at scale, the vast financial and network differences between the other students and me. When you are sitting next to somebody and their name sounds familiar and you wonder why. Oh, because their parents are always in *Harvard Magazine* about the millions of dollars they give to the school. Or you sit next to someone whose family started a law firm in New York as a Jewish family because they were discriminated against and prevented from getting a job at other WASP firms. You are classmates with people whose parents are partners at elite law firms, and you are the first person in your family to attend law school. As an FGBT professional, you start seeing this gap and you realize that you have no idea how to manage corporate culture, let alone the corporate culture of a law firm, let alone the corporate culture of East Coast law firms.

My fellow classmates at Harvard Law—not all of them, but some of them—grew up steeped in affluent, white European culture. We all go on yachting trips during our summer associate clerkships, but they know what to do, what the terminology is, how to participate, how to *be*. They tell stories about being at the yacht club as a kid. They know the acronyms and can tell inside jokes. They know all the cultural cues about etiquette and they have never been the misfit at a corporate outing. They know that you wear a blazer on the weekend at work events, not a suit. They know how many drinks to have at a cocktail party, how you hold the drink in your left hand so you can shake hands with your right hand. They know whether you can show up at a party late or whether you have to be there at a specific time, and whether you should bring a gift or not. They know the precise timing of how long a story should last, how risqué the punchline can be, and what questions to ask ("How's the family?" is the universal rapport builder at cocktail parties, it seems). All of these cultural cues are obvious to people who grew up somewhat privileged, but not obvious when you don't grow up in that environment.

I went directly from college to law school and then directly into the workforce, so I understood pretty quickly that I needed to figure out this cultural stuff. I did not want to be caught unaware; I did not want to be the misfit at the party, so I tried to master the art and science of cultural alignment in business. Part of the reason I became a mentor was because I sensed that a lot of people of color didn't know any of these cultural cues, so I decided I needed to tell all my friends, because I knew they were as clueless as I was. The FGBT professionals of color are at a huge disadvantage when it comes to all the nonbusiness, non-skills-based parts of corporate America, and a lot of them, like me, had to figure out this on their own. While there is no doubt some of my white friends had to learn it as well, almost all of my Black friends, Hispanic/Latine friends, and Asian American friends had to learn it, too.

Now that you have been introduced to FGBT professionals of color, let's dive a bit deeper into this cohort of employees. Specifically, I have identified four core value systems within the FGBT community. Almost always, these professionals are meritocratically qualified, have high ambition, a lack of sponsorship where they work, and have a tension between social impact and commercial outcomes within their careers. Understanding these value systems can prove vital in your efforts to recruit and retain these professionals.

Meritocratically Qualified

One way to spot FGBTs is by their résumés. They are almost always highly credentialed, both academically and professionally. These Gen X and Millennial professionals grew up in a post–Civil Rights era (1970–2000) where Black and brown folks were making spectacular, trailblazing achievements in politics, business, sports, entertainment, and the social sector. I was born in 1970 and came of age when Jesse Jackson ran for president of the United States, David Dinkins was mayor of New York, Oprah Winfrey and Bob Johnson were building billion-dollar media companies, and Michael Jordan and Magic Johnson were diversifying their fortunes beyond sports. As I witnessed these amazing achievements, I was encouraged by my parents and teachers and mentors that, with hard work, delayed gratification, and talent, I too could take my place among the ranks of these uber-successful leaders of color.

With this unshakeable belief in meritocracy, many of us succeeded in mostly white high schools and colleges and graduate schools, and almost certainly entered majority white places of work. We believed our talents and achievements would be enough. We built amazing résumés with

23

national scholarships, high honors from prestigious schools, and sky-high grade point averages. What separates this generation from previous generations of professionals of color is that we entered white workplaces en masse starting around the 1990s. Many of our parents and grandparents were successful in blue-collar or social service or small business endeavors, but few of us had successful family members with significant experience in corporate America. In that way, we were blazing new paths in this foreign landscape, confident we were qualified to be there.

I remember joining the speech and debate team at my all-Black high school. We were one of a handful of Black high schools competing in this overwhelmingly white extracurricular activity in New Orleans and throughout Louisiana. Perhaps 20 years prior, in a segregated Louisiana, we would not have even been allowed to compete against white students. And perhaps 20 years later, we would not have had the intense motivation to compete and win in these tournaments. But in the 1980s, we felt especially compelled to show we could win against our white competitors. Indeed, we took a special pride in being from an all-Black school and winning first place as a team in 11 of 13 statewide tournaments. We worked hard. We were qualified. And we won. There is nothing more FGBT than beating white folks at something in which they perhaps do not expect us to be competitive.

It is also worth noting that the FGBT professional's belief in meritocracy tends to be most ripe in the beginning or middle of their careers, before microaggressions, apathy, or outright racism dull their belief in the fairness of the system. As a result, your entry-level and middle managers of color tend to have more faith and belief that their merits will triumph them in the corporate tournament. As we will detail later, it is important to harness this optimism (via early and specific performance feedback, for instance) as early as possible to sustain these professionals through the inevitable valleys in their careers.

High on Ambition

With their belief in meritocracy and their gilded résumés, FGBT professionals tend to have higher aspirations than their white counterparts. In a 2022 study—"Women in the Workplace Report"—by McKinsey & Company and LeanIn.org, it was noted:

> "Black women leaders are more ambitious than other women at their level: 59 percent of Black women leaders want to be top executives, compared to 49 percent of women leaders overall. But they are also more likely than women leaders of other races and ethnicities to receive signals that it will be harder for them to advance," the report finds. "Compared to other women at their level, Black women leaders are more likely to have colleagues question their competence and to be subjected to demeaning behavior—and one in three Black women leaders says they have been denied or passed over for opportunities because of personal characteristics, including their race and gender."[3]

I can attest that at every company I have ever worked, I have wanted to be the CEO. As I sized up my mostly white and male competition, I was never dissuaded against whether I could stack up against them. With a couple of organizations, I came to have grave doubts about whether my spectacular performance and ethics would be recognized as such, but I never suffered any lack of confidence in my abilities versus my peers. On one episode of Protégé Podcast, I interviewed a classmate from Harvard Law. I asked him why he would launch an entrepreneurial venture while he was in a cushy leadership job at Viacom. He noted: "Once I realized I was not on track to be CEO of Viacom, there was no point in staying at the company." I found it fascinating that a Black executive making $500,000+ per year would walk away from a salary that put him in the top 2% of all

American earners to launch a business with no guarantee of such income. In his view, he was not going to be CEO, so it was time to leave.

I think this all-or-nothing phenomenon exists within FGBT professionals perhaps because we lack the generations of corporate role models in our families. Perhaps if my classmate were a third-generation corporate executive at a Fortune 500 company, he would understand the benefits of that level of financial privilege. He might have an aunt who had a spectacular summer home built from the stock options of a 30-year corporate career. He might have had a grandfather who had an endowed scholarship at a tony independent school and thus understood what that privilege meant to his grandson when he attended that school. But without that generational perspective, my friend, like many FGBT professionals, has an all-or-nothing approach to his career in corporate. Or maybe, as someone inspired by the Sean Combs and Rihannas of the world, he only aspires to be the CEO of whatever organization he works for, whether his own venture or Viacom.

Another reason could be that my classmate looked at the senior leadership team at Viacom and saw no one more qualified (and likely few equally qualified) than him, a Harvard College and Harvard Law graduate. I have interviewed and mentored hundreds of FGBT who felt the same. They chafed under the bizarro scenario where they were constantly asked to jump through hoops to prove their value when their less-qualified white counterparts got a pass. This is something I have experienced in my own career. When I left one majority white company to join another one, my boss asked me why the company could not retain African American talent. I was hesitant to respond to the question because I wondered whether he was ready for the brutal honesty his question required. I demurred, but he signaled an openness to a frank conversation. I told him: "The Black professionals at the firm are way more qualified than many of our white counterparts. We are asked to genuflect to prove our worthiness here and the truth is that this is the least impressive group of people most of us have ever been around." I was right; my soon-to-be former boss was not ready for that level of candor. The look on his face suggested that he never for once assumed that Black people thought some of their white colleagues were intellectually and professionally inferior. As highly ambitious FGBT professionals at the firm, most of us thought exactly that.

Lack of Sponsorship

With impeccable qualifications, belief in meritocracy, and ambition, FGBT professionals of color would probably be the first horses to bet on in the tournament for senior management at American companies, right? Unfortunately, that is not the case.

According to "The State of Black Women in Corporate America," a 2020 study:

> "Black women are much less likely than their non-Black colleagues to interact with senior leaders at work. This lack of access is mirrored in a lack of sponsorship: less than a quarter of Black women feel they have the sponsorship they need to advance their career. It also means Black women are less likely to be included in important conversations about company priorities and strategy, and they have fewer opportunities to get noticed by people in leadership."[4]

And according to a 2022 study by Recruiting Daily, the situation is bad for both Black women and men: "More than half of Black Americans, 55%, say they've never had a career mentor, according to a survey by the non-profit Jobs for the Future. According to the survey, almost half of Black Americans, 45%, said they have consulted either a formal or informal mentor at some point. Of those, 77% said their mentors shared the same race or ethnicity, a commonality they found useful."[5] A 2020 IBM report, "Untapped Potential: The Hispanic Talent Advantage," found that

41% of the Hispanic executives surveyed say they have benefited from formal mentoring and on-the-job training.[6] That means nearly 60% had no formal mentoring or training or didn't benefit from it.

I think you get the picture here.

So why are professionals of color mentored and sponsored less than their white counterparts? In a word: risk. Professionals of color are seen as a risk to be mentored or sponsored because senior leaders in companies and organizations want their advice and counsel to help executives win in the corporate tournament. And these senior leaders, consciously or unconsciously, know that white men are more likely to be promoted and to take their eventual place in the ranks of senior leadership. I simply don't buy the idea that senior white men mentor younger white men only because they have social affinity with them. I have seen too much evidence of white men crossing lines of class, orientation, and personality to go out of their way to mentor white men who they had little in common with other than their white maleness. I think white men mentor white men because they are making bets on who will win the corporate tournament. And based on the fact that white men overindex in leadership roles in corporate America against their demographic makeup in the country, these white men believe they are betting correctly.

I once helped develop a mentor protégé program at a company. The data from the company's previous mentoring initiatives showed a clear preference among white men, the power brokers at the company, to mentor younger white men. Not the strong performers at the company, the white men. So we suggested changes. We had mentors and protégés complete surveys as if they were on a dating app. We received data about who the strong performers were. And then we matched the strong performing protégés with an executive mentor who shared some core values and interests. Know what happened? All of the matches were a success. Years later, the company revealed to me that, for quite a few women of color in particular, these mentor/protégé matches were transformational. Women of color in the program were promoted at a higher rate than white men. Some had changed departments and had made incredible impact in their new functional or business groups. The novel but commonsense approach of breaking up the cabal of white male mentor/protégé relationships in favor of a more data-driven approach profoundly changed career outcomes for FGBT professionals of color at this company. And I bet it led to more white men mentoring young professionals from diverse backgrounds in the future without being prompted. We proved it wasn't so risky to mentor that young Filipino woman. It is like enjoying a pomegranate. Once you get over your biases, you find yourself opened up to an entirely new and positive experience.

The Tension Between Social Impact and Commercial Outcomes

Another hallmark of FGBT talent is the tension between succeeding in the corporate tournament and making a social impact. Sandwiched between the tremendous success of corporate leaders like former Xerox CEO Ursula Burns, former American Express CEO Ken Chenault, and Vista Capital founder and CEO Robert Smith are the murders of Breonna Taylor, George Floyd, and Tyre Nichols. FGBT professionals of color can find staying on a corporate career path to be lonely and unfulfilling. The ever-present thought bubble over the heads of FGBT talent is "What am I doing to help my community?" We will discuss later in the book how to harness this instinct, but let's first understand how deep this sentiment is among FGBT professionals of color. Typically, an FGBT employee makes several conscious levels of inquiry to understand whether their current job at their current employer helps them make the impact they desire. I think there are three levels of analysis in this decision-making process.

The first layer of this analysis is figuring out what their employer is doing in terms of DEI. Is it meaningful and authentic or reactionary and superficial? Is the DEI strategy sustainable, or is it dependent on the superstar chief diversity officer's demands on senior leadership? And by now, every senior executive should expect that professionals of color know chapter and verse about the company's track record on discrimination and racism at the company, with its marketing, and with its product/service development and roll out. FGBT employees discuss these matters via Slack or text among other FGBTs and they go on Black Twitter and chime in anonymously and read about their employer's boneheaded moves.

The second layer of analysis is for FGBT professionals to figure out what they are doing in their own individual role to make a meaningful social impact. I have a long-time friend who now leads a foundation for a multinational delivery services company. She worked for several years as a lobbyist for the company but found the work largely unfulfilling. Through her work with frontline staff, she uncovered the startling reality that these delivery professionals often witnessed acts of human trafficking at the homes where they dropped off packages. During my conversations with her, she often wondered how she could make that particular issue—ending human trafficking—part of her day job. Fiercely committed to this cause, she seriously considered leaving the company to take a job at a nonprofit. With some advocacy and mentorship, she finally made it happen. Five years after our conversation, she leads the company's corporate foundation, and one of their major initiatives is ending human trafficking. My friend was not only retained by the company an extra five years and counting, but she is now making a tremendous difference for people who are victims, or who are at risk, of human trafficking.

It is, however, unrealistic to think that every professional of color will have an opportunity to carve out a unique professional niche like this that matches their personal values. For most FGBT staff, working within employee resource groups (ERGs) can provide a community of kindred spirits who share similar cultural values, traditions, and longings to socially impact their communities in a positive way. This is a third layer of analysis for FGBT regarding whether they can actualize their social impact aspirations at their company. ERGs do wonderful things like paint schools in underserved communities, mentor underserved students, partner with and donate funds to Black, Hispanic/Latine, Asian American, and Indigenous nonprofits. In doing so, they boost the morale of FGBT staff of color and increase the likelihood of a company retaining them. ERGs provide such an easy win for companies that I don't understand why every company over 250 employees does not actively encourage the formation of these internal groups. I once worked at a company where the culture was so toxic that women and people of color actively desired to launch ERG groups but were afraid it would send the wrong signal to management. There is more to sustaining a thriving ERG group than simply launching one, including tying the ERG group's mission to business priorities, interesting and meaningful programming, a culture of trust and transparency, and executive sponsorship. But companies will not—and do not need to—get all of this right out of the gate. Launching an ERG group can provide a simple way to connect with the values of your FGBT talent.

With all of these challenges, there is still one (at least one) more issue to consider. These amazing FGBT professionals, qualified and ambitious, who are resisting the urge of entrepreneurship, who are aligned with your company's value and mission, are still going to be hard to recruit and retain for one simple reason: *they are in high demand.* It is worth emphasizing and explaining this further. Talented and credentialed diverse leaders exist in every function and industry in the market. Among the usual senior leadership roles in legal, finance, operations, and marketing, the following positions are the roles we have recruited for clients and where we have delivered diverse slates of candidates:

- Chief Economist
- Chief Advancement Officer
- Chief Investment Officer
- Chief Information Officer
- Head of Sales Solutions
- Managing Director, Data Strategy

In my over 20 years of executive recruiting, I have never recruited for a role where I could not deliver a qualified slate of diverse candidates. And yes, I might think I am the world's best diversity recruiter, but the truth is also that these executives exist in every function and business imaginable. *If you have an FGBT executive who is performing well, gels within your culture, and seems to be upbeat and positive about their tenure at the company, you should do whatever it takes to retain them.* And you should do so because of their relative rarity. Rare things are usually more expensive. They are usually desirable in the broader market by others. And when you put that rarity in a professional, they tend to know that they are special. After all, recruiters like me are likely calling them about other opportunities all the time.

I once managed a recruiting project for a fast-growing company in Silicon Valley. This company had about $1 billion in revenue and was seeking a head of sales solutions. An incredibly talented African American woman had reached out to me several months prior to the launch of the search seeking career advice. She worked at a prominent technology company and was wondering what her next career move might be. I remembered that she wanted something with strategy and sales in her next role, which would fast track her to the C-suite. I reached out to her to discuss this opportunity with our client, and she agreed that it met her litmus test for her next role. After her first-round interview with our client, I set up a call to provide feedback.

"When can I meet the CEO of the company?" she asked. I hesitated because the CEO was not going to be on the interview list. I was sure she would likely meet the CEO after she accepted the offer, and certainly within her first 30 days at the company, but he was not on the interview list. I relayed all of this to her but told her I would ask the client if a meeting with the CEO was possible. She replied: "I'm asking because the CEO [of a Fortune 20 technology company] came on the Zoom interview I had last week and asked me what it would take to get me at the company." Not only did the CEO interrupt a Zoom interview in a half-court shot of recruiting, but the offer the company suggested was double her current salary, and 40% higher than the most aggressive compensation package my client could offer. Not surprisingly, she took the job with the big tech company.

The recruiting overtures we at Protégé Search make to highly qualified executive leaders of color are frequent and intense. When I do an executive search and the candidate is one of these rare executives who has exceptional credentials, spectacular successes at their company, and a tenure longer than five years, I know it is going to take an opportunity of a lifetime to get them to leave that company. I cannot just offer higher compensation or title on behalf of my client. I have to make a cogent and compelling case about why the inflection point in their career matches perfectly with this business need at the company. I know I am not only competing with what should be a strong retention play by their employer, but also with the future executive roles that will come their way by other executive recruiting firms. How we approach cultivating relationships with passively interested diverse talent is to treat them like the superstars that they are. We approach them understanding their rarity—and understanding that, they, too, are aware of their rarity—and treating them with the respect they deserve.

When I was leaving another corporate job, my boss again asked me why I was leaving. "We have such a difficult time retaining African American professionals, so I'd love to hear your thoughts on what we can do better in this area," he said. I was very hesitant about answering him honestly and wanted to just give a perfunctory exit interview with the standard rom-com breakup mantra: "It's not you, it's me." But that would have been a lie. It was them. It was the culture of the company, the horrible way I was either ignored or harshly treated, the daily microaggressions and, in some cases, overt racism I experienced. I again summoned the courage to be a truth teller and gave my soon-to-be former boss the unvarnished truth. "I think the senior white leaders of the firm feel like Black professionals should feel lucky to work here. It's reflected in the overall culture of the firm and how people are recruited, promoted, and paid. Yet, it's the professionals of color who have the Ivy League degrees and the graduate degrees. Our white supervisors have the state school degrees but come from wealthy families. We are overqualified, yet under-leveled when it comes to title and compensation. We are getting calls all the time from recruiters who offer 50% more money for similar roles. Most of us take these interviews because we think 'it can't be worse than working here'; at least I'll make more money," I said (with the confidence of someone with a brand-new job).

My boss's jaw was almost on the ground. I think he kept a centimeter length gap between his lips for most of my little sermon about The Overqualified Blacks at Mediocre Company. I told him that the firm should hire the white *and* Black talent from Georgia State and Bowling Green, and not hire Blacks from the Ivy League and whites from state schools. I do not know if he took my advice. There are still highly qualified Black professionals at that company and there are still highly qualified white professionals there, too, but there are a whole lot of exceptionally mediocre white people there with résumés that no professional of color could even get an interview with. This matters in recruiting because my new employer treated me like a rockstar throughout the recruiting process. I had an identified sponsor, was given VIP treatment to their events and programs, and was ensured I would be on a fast track to even more significant leadership opportunities beyond the role they had custom developed for me. Is it any wonder that I left that other company?

Now that you have perhaps a fuller and more nuanced understanding about these ambitious, qualified, and highly sought-after professionals and executives who are resisting the lure of entrepreneurship and the option of quiet quitting, it is time to think through the strategies you can implement to recruit and retain them.

PART II

WHAT TO DO ABOUT IT

With a solid understanding of the psyche of FGBT professionals of color and the role your company's reputation plays in the strategy to recruit diverse talent, you might be ready to launch (or relaunch) a new diversity recruiting initiative. Well, not so fast. Your company almost assuredly has a strategy on recruiting talent, and possibly even an approach for recruiting diverse talent or an overall DEI strategy. Your newly inspired efforts likely will have to be incorporated into an existing talent acquisition/management framework or DEI strategy. I have found that a lot of companies are trying to do something on diversity recruiting, but much of what they are doing is not working well. Yet, they persist in maintaining a flawed and mediocre process.

In this next section, I will detail the frameworks, processes, and philosophies undergirding most diversity recruiting strategies at companies and large, complex nonprofit organizations. These are some of the things that companies have to *stop* doing if they want to be successful in recruiting diverse talent in a sustainable manner. In terms of HR strategies and processes, these are some of the dead leaves you'll have to prune and the weeds you'll have to remove to create the fertile ground for your diversity recruiting efforts to grow.

CHAPTER TWO

STOP DOING THIS: Not Recognizing the Phase of DEI Adoption Your Organization Is In

I have decades of executive search and recruiting experience, first with a global organization and now with my own company, Protégé Search, and over those decades I have figured out that there are four phases of adoption for companies seeking successful DEI outcomes, each with its own challenges and issues. As I mentioned in the introduction, I did not write this book to convince you that DEI is a good thing, because if you do not believe that diversity is a key to innovation, growth, and adaptability at this point, you may not want the status quo to change at your organization. But if companies could imagine their most commercially successful versions of themselves as happening on the opposite end of their DEI journeys, they would be much more willing to embrace these strategies.

If the PGA Tour, which had a "Whites Only" clause until 1961,[1] knew what the PGA Tour would look like if it integrated and allowed Black players and the Tiger Woodses of the world to play in tournaments, they would have integrated a long time ago. Tiger Woods brought millions of people into the golf world—millions of people buying equipment, clothing, shoes, and rounds of golf. He catalyzed millions of people to take lessons, join golf clubs, vacation at golf resorts, watch golf on TV, and spend their hard-earned dollars on the sport. And what does the PGA Tour think about DEI now? Well, it is dying to find the next Tiger Woods, the next superstar who can appeal to the multicultural millions and expand the sport to a new generation of fans. The PGA Tour has tasted the commercial success of diversity and its senior executives are now strong advocates of DEI.

The PGA Tour represents an organization that went from a relatively cold embrace of DEI in the 1970s to true believer status in the 1990s. The organization went from a Phase One to a Phase Three organization on DEI and we all saw it in real time. So, if you are thinking about diversity and you want to start that journey, then it is important to understand that there are different phases of the journey and that, for you or your company to be able to harness the power of diversity, there are fundamental processes you need to put in place. The idea is not to diversify for diversity's sake, but to make diversity instrumental to the strategic and operational aspects of an organization. The four-phase framework is a simple but powerful tool to help you pinpoint the reality of your current situation, help you think about what parts are missing or what gaps you might have, and provide some guidance on what the next steps for you might be. I also highlight some of the mistakes I have seen companies make that prevent them from creating critical momentum or getting to a tipping point with their DEI efforts.

This simple four-phase framework is not philosophically framed like an anti-racist strategy, which you should also consider implementing within your organization. And it is not based on the latest cutting-edge anti-bias research that you might incorporate into your DEI strategy. This four-phase model is a straightforward baseline framework for how your enterprise can evolve on DEI. You should feel free to augment this model with specific philosophically and culturally relevant content and strategies that might work best for your organization. There are, of course, other impactful DEI frameworks your company can consider implementing via the many DEI strategy consulting firms out there.

PHASE ONE: YOU NEED A DEI STRATEGY, BUT DON'T HAVE ANYTHING IN PLACE

The Phase One company has the intention to make a big push into diversity but does not know how to do it. They do not know how to recruit and retain people of color (POC), they do not have an enterprise-wide competency in diversity, and so they never get any momentum. And it is not from lack of trying, because the Phase One company typically has tried something around diversity in fits and starts. They have had an evangelist, an apostle, a leader who has taken diversity seriously, but that person left the company because they did not have funding, or they could not get company-wide support, or they lost enthusiasm with the slow pace of change. They were the canary in the coalmine, and when that person leaves, there is a giant void left behind where people think, "Wow, we should be more diverse in our senior leadership team or in our staff," but nobody knows how to do it.

The Phase One company comes to Protégé Search and says, "What should we do?" Our approach at Protégé is to literally put in place a lot of these Pomegranate Principles and methodologies so they at least have a framework for doing the initial activities to be successful in recruiting and retaining talent. Because it is easy for people to think, "Oh, I can start recruiting diverse talent, I can get this going on my own." Really? So, what are you going to do in terms of your interview process—the same as you did before? Most companies think that, if they just aim to include more diverse talent, that will be sufficient to achieve the outcome. And of course, that never achieves it because your interview team and your recruiting team are not diverse. You do not have partnerships with diversity recruiting firms. You do not have partnerships with the talent market, with the National Black MBA Association, and you do not have relationships with Howard University, or Spelman, or Morehouse or any HBCUs. You just have good intentions that never get any traction; that does not move the needle. And what winds up happening is that the five white recruiters try to corral one or two Black or Hispanic/Latine people for the candidate slate so they can check the box on diversity. Those candidates may or may not work; they may or may not be qualified; they may or may not be interested or, even if they are interested, they may not be well-cultivated as candidates. And these diverse professionals you somehow got onto the slate? They almost always withdraw as candidates. And the company will say, "Well, we tried."

A Phase One company is often at the stage where there is the ghost of some failed activities, but there is not really the spirit of DEI in the culture, and therefore, diversity, equity, and inclusion are not enterprise-wide values. So, while we are often called in to help with a recruiting project, we do more than just find a candidate because we want to help pave the way for all the other things a client has to do to make sure that it is successful in diversity recruiting. At a minimum, before you even approach diverse talent as part of a recruiting strategy, a Phase One company ought to get the following processes in place:

- Launch an ERG group for professionals of color.
- Conduct diversity/unconscious bias training across the organization.
- Create a diversity hiring goal.

A Phase One company that can put together elementary fundamentals into their overall talent acquisition processes can get a DEI recruiting initiative started and build from there. Like any change leadership initiative, success metrics should be based on early adoption and momentum for the new process. The worse thing a company can do in Phase One is overpromise and underdeliver. With some enthusiasm around early success, you can build a more robust platform from there.

PHASE TWO: YOU HAVE A DEI STRATEGY, BUT IT IS NOT SUSTAINABLE

A Phase Two company is the most common of all companies in trying to foster DEI because these companies have started their diversity and inclusion journey, they want to maintain it, but they realize somewhat reluctantly that these processes have not taken root in the organization. Or the strategy worked for a year or two, but then a recession hit, and everyone put DEI on the back burner. These kinds of companies need more significant support, and even though they have correctly identified the crux of the problem as recruitment and retention, they need help building an infrastructure that will make their company more diverse and inclusive over the various seasons of an enterprise.

Most Phase Two companies have a chief diversity officer (CDO). According to a 2022 study by McKinsey & Company, 53% of Fortune 500 companies have an executive leading DEI efforts.[2] I am going to safely guess that the 47% that do not have a CDO are Phase One companies. These companies almost always have the processes of Phase One companies in place and a few other initiatives. In addition to some recruiting infrastructure and partnerships and hiring goals, ERG groups, and a CDO, Phase Two companies typically have another function or two associated with DEI. DEI starts to not just be a single pillar associated with human resources, but is a multifunctional approach spread across multiple parts of the enterprise. Phase Two organizations typically have the following infrastructure:

- A senior executive charged with managing the DEI strategy.
- A public commitment to DEI manifest on almost all official organizational copy, including the website, annual reports, signage inside offices, etc.
- A relatively diverse talent acquisition team.
- Some aspirational goals associated with DEI (application of The Rooney Rule, 50% diversity on slates, etc.).
- Successful partnerships with HBCUs, Hispanic/Latine and Native American–serving institutions, and other organizations focused on diverse talent.

After George Floyd was murdered, there was significant activity around DEI and hundreds of companies established or accelerated their DEI processes. From a practitioner perspective, I saw companies try to skip one or two phases in their DEI adoption. But many companies settled in Phase Two or Phase Three (outlined later in this chapter). Why? Because these middle phases of DEI adoption are relatively easy to migrate to because they involve new programs, new processes, and new funding. After the thousands of town hall meetings with Black and other employees of color, after commitments to fund racial justice programs, and after the pledges to diversify their workforces, most American companies and organizations felt like they had updated and modernized their DEI strategies to meet the dynamics of unpredictable new external realities and a vocal and socially conscious employee population.

Many times, when we recruit a senior executive for a company in Phase Two, the hiring executive—the head of HR or the CEO—will select a person of color as the placement executive. (We only guarantee a diverse slate; it is up to the company to make their own informed choice among those candidates.) When that executive is going to be the only person of color in the C-suite, for instance, it creates a unique challenge for us as a recruiting firm. In this case, we have to make sure that executive wants to be a trailblazer within that culture. We look for that competency in the candidate and evaluate whether they have been a trailblazer in another company. Have you been the only one or the first one? Have they integrated within the C-suite? Because the role of a trailblazer is unique. There is a lot of scrutiny on the executive and they need to have a competency of performing while under tremendous pressure. That person needs to have significant emotional fortitude and resilience and a great support structure (typically from peer mentors), which augment their sense of possible isolation in the organization. All the trailblazers in sports and other professions had a strong support structure undergirding their trailblazing careers. Everyone knows the story of Jackie Robinson, who broke Major League Baseball's color barrier, but behind the scenes there was Branch Rickey who helped pave the way for Robinson and helped him succeed within the league. Leaders can be functionally brilliant, technically expert, but if they do not have the support system that can help them succeed as one of the only persons of color, then typically they are not going to perform well in that environment.

I once recruited a chief information officer for a company. The CEO was very pleased with the search process and ready to welcome his CIO, a woman with extensive expertise in the function. I mentioned to him that it would be a good idea to make sure he reserved 20% of her time for her trailblazer duties. The CEO seemed puzzled by this description. I noted that we had not only just recruited the most senior woman at the company, but one of the most senior women in the industry. I said: "Every woman inside of this company, and plenty outside of it, are going to want to be mentored by her; she is going to be invited to be on the boards of women's leadership organizations and companies as well." The CEO, a Caucasian man, never thought about that reality. Had he selected a white male for the role, it is doubtful there would be those kinds of expectations put on the executive. But with a woman trailblazer, it was almost a certainty.

The biggest challenge for Phase Two companies is the reluctance of those on the front lines of DEI adoption—the directors and vice presidents of the organization—who are sufficiently removed from the C-suite (where DEI may be considered a core enterprise strategy), but who are nonetheless possessed of enough power as hiring managers to dilute DEI strategies. We will cover these efforts to thwart DEI in greater detail later in this chapter, but one of the reasons Phase Two companies don't evolve into Phase Three companies is the unchecked and quiet rebellion of mainly white middle managers against DEI strategies.

PHASE THREE: YOU HAVE SOME MOMENTUM AND SUCCESS WITH DEI, BUT RISKS REMAIN

The Phase Three company's DEI strategy is operating like a well-oiled machine. With robust infrastructure in place and more enterprise-wide adoption than resistance, the Phase Three company looks like, from the outside, the model organization for DEI. Phase Three companies rarely appear in the media with racism or discrimination controversies, and they typically have more than one person of color in senior leadership. In addition to these elements and much of the infrastructure in Phases One and Two, Phase Three companies on DEI have evolved to incorporate the following features and attributes:

- Diversity on the board of directors.
- A chief diversity officer function with a budget and requisite staff.
- A pipeline of internal succession candidates for management level roles.
- A four-pronged approach to DEI with robust initiatives in HR, supplier diversity, marketing, and public affairs and philanthropic giving.
- Deep and mutually beneficial relationships with leaders in civil rights and advocacy organizations associated with communities of color.
- Measurable goals and outcomes tied to DEI initiatives, including compensation of senior leaders tied to DEI.

Phase Three companies typically have not only robust DEI programs and processes, but they have tasted the commercial success from these efforts. Disney is a great example of a Phase Three company. Disney is not only concerned about marketing to a global audience with its theme parks, resorts, and cruises, it has to think about the content it produces through its media platforms, which include ESPN and ABC. My brother has worked at ESPN for 22 years. While he has not described it as a perfect enterprise, he has largely found the company to be progressive on DEI issues. This is coming from one of the media giant's top anchors who has waded into controversial racial topics, including ESPN's hiring of Rush Limbaugh and the controversy surrounding NFL quarterback Colin Kaepernick's protest about police brutality. I have never worked for Disney and Disney has never been a client of our firm, but I am going to make an educated guess that Disney understands at an enterprise level the business case around DEI, and that their efforts do not come exclusively from some notion that DEI is the right thing to do.

There are two big risks that often exist in Phase Three companies. First, there is the risk of institutional complacency. A couple of years of climbing the rankings in Fair360's annual list of the most diverse companies and recognition from *Working Mother* might signal to earnest leaders in the organization that some great chasm of DEI adoption has been crossed. Companies can be especially vulnerable to this overconfidence if all of this DEI infrastructure came in the aftermath of some unsettling racial discrimination lawsuit or the public shame stemming from a racism controversy. Public awards for diversity can be a salve to the battered and bruised institutional ego of a company rocked to its core from a diversity crisis. Many companies and organizations make the mistake of resting on their new DEI laurels.

The second risk of the Phase Three company is that the advocacy for DEI adoption rests with a few powerful executives at the organization. These leaders are the executives who sponsor the LGBTQ ERG group. They are the ones painting the walls of the inner city school during the company's corporate social responsibility outing. They are mentoring the superstar leaders of color who get promotions and who are profiled in *Black Enterprise*. What happens when these DEI evangelists leave the company? What happens to that sponsorship and advocacy? Many times, organizations experience a significant shift or stalled momentum in their DEI initiatives as a result. These organizations have much of the right DEI infrastructure in place, but they are missing a core enterprise-wide principle with the strategy: sustainability.

PHASE FOUR: YOU HAVE A SUSTAINABLE AND INTEGRATED DEI STRATEGY

The Phase Four company on DEI represents the most well-evolved enterprise in their industries and even the economy. These organizations have been on a DEI journey for at least a decade and many times for a few decades. They have been stuck at Phase One, plowed their way to get to Phase Two, rested but didn't get totally complacent in Phase Three, and ultimately arrived at Phase Four. A Phase Four organization on DEI has all of the Phase Three elements and also includes a rare output from any change management initiative: sustainability. **Sustainability with DEI means that the strategy is so well-integrated into the culture and processes of the organization that it is a normal part of doing business.** DEI becomes like IT at a company. When the CIO leaves for a new job, she doesn't take all of the laptops with her and shut down the cloud computing storage with all the company's data. She doesn't because IT is an integral part of how that company does business; it is not subject to any executive's tenure with the company. DEI in its most sustainable form operates like that: strategic, resilient, and embedded in the operations.

I had an experience of witnessing a function being completely embedded within a company's culture and its operations. A utility company invited us to discuss recruiting their chief diversity officer position via a Zoom call. After we exchanged pleasantries, the utility company executive started the business part of the meeting with this: "Our company values safety and it is one of our most important values. And before we get started, I want us to do a quick safety check around our home office setups." I am thinking, is this guy serious? And he was dead serious. And there were five of us on a call and we looked down at our wires and connections and he said, "How are we doing?" and I responded, "I'm doing okay, but I should probably get a better surge protector because I'm really only using a power strip right now." And he said, "Where is that power strip situated?" and I said, "Well, it's on top of this woven rug." The executive said, "Rory, that's a fire hazard. I'm going to ask you to move that off the rug right now." And I am thinking, are we doing this right now? This guy is telling me how to set up my home office. And so, he said, "You know, that's how important safety is. We are a utility company, so electrical fires happen like this all time, and people are getting injured in their homes because they're working in hastily constructed home offices, which are not set up like a typical corporate office environment."

The point of me telling that story is that this utility company had their safety strategy embedded inside the institution at a granular level. I was not talking to the chief safety officer or the SVP of compliance. I was talking to a guy who worked in human resources and who was telling a potential vendor to check his electric cords in his home office. He doesn't know me from Adam. I thought to myself, who is responsible for that safety protocol? It sounds like *everybody* at the utility company is responsible for that safety protocol. It is my hope that, at some point, diversity, equity, and inclusion will be shared that way in companies. I can envision a day where somebody will ask me at the top of a meeting, "Hi Rory, you should know that diversity, equity, and inclusion are important values in our company, and I want to start right now by asking you: Have you been inclusive of all of your diverse stakeholders in your company's strategy and operational goals this week?"

A great example of a Phase Four company is the National Basketball Association. The NBA has incredible diversity in senior leadership. It has exceptional relationships with external Black, Hispanic/Latine, and Asian American nonprofits and advocacy organizations. It measures and incentivizes DEI outcomes through a rigorous performance management system. And most notably, DEI is a first principles value system that all stakeholders associated with the league embrace.

How did the NBA get this way? The NBA did two things early on that other sports leagues were reticent to do: 1) it embraced the culture of players from diverse backgrounds, and 2) it internationalized the game. You might recall the 1990s era of the NBA when the league grappled with how to manage and market a new generation of spectacular tattooed talent like Allen Iverson and Latrell Sprewell. Hip-hop became the stadium anthems at NBA games. Around this same time, players like Tony Kukoc and Dirk Nowitski were becoming household names among NBA fans. Other leagues had long had Black and Hispanic/Latine players from the inner city and international players as superstars, but no league embraced urban culture and internationalism like the NBA.

As our firm has expanded into Europe, I recently traveled to Paris, Amsterdam, Berlin, and Lisbon over the course of six months. In each of these European capitals, I heard American hip-hop being played in the most tony hotels, restaurants, and cafes. Black/urban music and culture are considered the epitome of what is cool and hip and these upscale establishments unabashedly embraced that culture. It is as if the NBA predicted the future of urban being a proxy for cool, and that technology (which they also embraced early) would connect us and make the world feel like a much smaller place.

When we work with a Phase Four company, they are only looking for highly sought-after candidates, and these candidates are not even going to consider a company if that company does not have their act together on DEI. We have to have a different approach to recruiting for a Phase Four company than we do for one for Phase One. For Phase One we try to convince somebody, "Hey, I think you can be the trailblazer here. I think you can make a big impact; you can be the catalyst to start this new wave of executive hiring. You will be a mentor and hero to dozens of employees at this company and people will look back and see your hiring and leadership as inflection points of positive, institutional change at the organization." A Phase Four company is already well-developed on DEI. The pitch to an executive of color to consider a Phase Four company is that the organization is a true meritocracy by how diverse it is, especially in senior management. You do not have to speak for all women or Black people or Indigenous people. As an executive in a Phase Four company, you can simply do your job. Moreover, you can do it with a special manner of pride in knowing that the culture of the organization is sustainably diverse, equitable, and inclusive.

I often am asked what the timeline is to go from a Phase One to a Phase Four organization—which is a great question. The short answer is at least a decade. I don't know if a company can go from Phase One to Phase Four in two or three years no matter how earnest or intentional. Metaphorically this is a marathon, not a sprint.

A hallmark of success for a Phase One company, for instance, is when a person of color in your executive leadership team is no longer an anomaly. The hallmark for an organization within Phase Four is, in contrast, when the leadership of the company is, or is tracking toward, being representative of the U.S. population. White men make up 30% of the American population according to the U.S. Census,[3] but account for about 85% of C-suite leadership roles, according to a Mercer study.[4] For a leadership team of 10 executives to reflect current demographics in the United States, there would need to be approximately three white men, three white women, two women of color, and two men of color. To be clear, this would mean *half* of the senior leadership team would be women and 40% of the team would be people of color. Companies and organizations can use other benchmarks for the makeup of the senior management team, such as the racial and ethnic percentage of business school graduates. The reality is that the current demographic makeup of leadership in corporate America and within many nonprofit and government organizations has no statistical relevance to anything meaningful or measurable other than, perhaps, the leadership histories of those organizations. What it means to be a Phase Four organization is to break away from meaningless traditions, and commit to having a leadership team which reflects the markets and communities you serve.

A Mission-Focused Path to Diversity

Planned Parenthood Federation of America is the best example I know of a nonprofit organization that transformed itself from largely nondiverse to a tremendously diverse organization. For decades, Planned Parenthood was run by almost exclusively white women, but over the last 15 years, they have made a concerted effort to recruit and retain men and women of color. Once Planned Parenthood reframed their mission to be more inclusive, to be not just about reproductive rights, but reproductive justice, it resonated with Latina and Black women. Now, the head of communications is Black; the head of HR is Black; the head of DEI is a Black male; the top policy leaders are Black; and the CEO is Black. This transformation might have been unthinkable 15 years ago.

Once leaders understand where they are on the DEI adoption scale, they can make sure they take the steps to evolve to the next phase until they become a Phase Four company. *Companies and organizations have to stop thinking of their DEI journey as a static state of affairs.* I have found that companies typically toggle between phases quite often, especially in turbulent moments in their industry or when the economy is in recession.

Let's turn to a few specific, additional measures organizations should stop doing if they want to foster best practices in DEI.

CHAPTER THREE

STOP DOING THIS: Relying on the Chief Diversity Officer Role to Solve Every DEI Problem

One of the other principal problems organizations have is an overreliance on the chief diversity officer to solve every DEI challenge. DEI is an institutional imperative and it is everyone's responsibility to operationalize the DEI strategy. Again, think about this like IT. Everyone has technology tools so the organization can be more collaborative, efficient, and innovative. It is not the chief information officer or chief technology officer's responsibility to deal with every single issue related to technology. Yes, you should call the IT help desk when your laptop doesn't start or when the Wi-Fi network is spotty on your floor. But to think that a single person is responsible for how all technology is used, for solving for every glitch, for absolving everyone in the enterprise of their responsibility to use technology responsibly in the workplace would be profoundly misguided and ineffective.

I think it is important to understand the history and nature of these important and complex roles so that we can understand how to use these incredibly talented, insightful, and committed executives and their teams appropriately.

THE CHIEF DIVERSITY OFFICER ROLE

I want to provide some context for the chief diversity officer role because many people do not realize that the role has been a part of corporate America since the 1970s. I think of the role as evolving in three distinct time periods or epochs: the compliance era; the chief diversity officer 2.0 era; and the post–George Floyd era. My own experience with chief diversity officer searches has been going on across at least two of these epochs and I have a long list of organizations where I have recruited their CDO or the chief human resources officer (who had full or partial responsibility for DEI), including The New York Times Company (twice), Harvard University, Princeton University, the NFL, Tapestry, Patagonia, Legal Services Corporation, Ben & Jerry's, the American Medical Association (during Covid), the American Red Cross (during Hurricane Katrina), Seagate Technology, and many others.

Not only has the CDO role changed considerably over the past 20 years, but there are some companies and organizations that maximize the impact of this role while many others allow these talented executives to flounder.

THE EVOLUTION OF THE CHIEF DIVERSITY OFFICER ROLE: 1970S TO TODAY

The CDO position largely came about in the 1980s and 1990s, and it grew out of a compliance function that began in the 1970s. Companies started appointing affirmative action compliance executives and those professionals monitored vendor relationships and the hiring of professionals and staff of color. The U.S. federal government, under President Richard Nixon, required oversight and reporting on affirmative action from all federal contractors. The role then grew from strictly compliance to a person who led multicultural affairs, a role that was an early precursor to the chief diversity officer position. Diversity moved beyond procurement and HR to designing strategies to sell and market products and services to a burgeoning Black and Hispanic/Latine middle class. This executive was responsible for pretty much all of the diversity programming inside of an organization, to be a sounding board for any issues or grievances people have inside the organization around racism or discrimination, to handle PR crises, and to manage any and all diversity initiatives. These professionals were typically individual contributors and, if they did have staff, they worked on compliance matters and reports.

And then in the 1980s and 1990s, we started seeing companies call this role the chief diversity officer. I have often called this period the evolution of "CDO 2.0." The role became much more complex and dynamic and this function now covered a lot of different areas, but the most robust and evolved of them included the following functional areas:

Supplier diversity: Sourcing and vetting diverse suppliers for the company's procurement processes.

Human resources: Recruiting, developing, and retaining diverse talent.

Philanthropic outreach: Managing the contributions and philanthropic outreach to organizations focused on communities of color.

Multicultural marketing: Creating strategies to market and sell products and services to distinct diverse segments of the economy.

In the most forward-thinking companies, the CDO played an outsized role across multiple domains. Then, as companies grew, they realized they needed a specialist in each of those areas managing some of those functions, but the CDO remained the chief strategist. The CDO almost always reported to the head of human resources and sometimes they reported to the organization's general counsel, especially when there was a big compliance function associated with the role. Occasionally, the CDO reported to the CEO, but that reporting relationship was rare, though it has been increasing in frequency in the post–George Floyd era.

Notwithstanding 50 years of diversity efforts in companies and organizations, the CDO role has evolved nearly as much since George Floyd's murder in 2020 as it has in all the years before. I believe the role has the potential to be a truly transformational function inside most organizations. It has hyperextended itself to be a much more complex function because, after George Floyd's murder, companies realized they had misread, or underappreciated, or underreported, or underresponded to the angst and the issues associated with their diverse stakeholders. And after George Floyd's murder, many companies started asking, "Well, what do we do?" And the first thing they did was hold town hall meetings and the CEO delivered a statement, largely drafted by the chief diversity officer. And it was a statement about the principles that they believed in, how horrific the George Floyd situation was, and, many times, a commitment to take action.

After these town hall meetings, or even during the meetings, companies started listening to what their employees were saying. And they heard an earful. Almost every CEO understood that what their employees of color were going through was much worse than they had imagined. POC employees were under much more stress, had far greater anxiety than others, and were much less supported than CEOs understood them to be. CEOs also got an earful about the microaggressions at work. They heard an earful about the lack of promotion opportunities inside the company. They heard that the company did not stand up or did not represent their values in many ways. And they heard that this had been happening for years, and in some sad cases, for decades. Professionals of color put a mirror to companies and organizations and asked: Where was the company when Philando Castile and Alton Sterling were murdered? Where was the company when a host of other Black people were murdered by police? Why was the company responding now?

These town hall meetings also underscored the point that there was not a lot of infrastructure in place to really address root-cause issues. Yes, companies had affinity groups organized around a particular ethnic group or shared interest (a women's association, LGBTQ affinity group, African American affinity group, and others), but there really wasn't core infrastructure to help them. And what CEOs and boards of directors came to realize is that they either underresourced the CDO function, or they had put inside the CDO function sole responsibility for solving all the problems related to race, inclusion, and belonging inside the organization, which is impossible. That is an important distinction to make and one of the most significant learnings coming out of the post–George Floyd era: *that the chief diversity officer is not going to be able to solve all of the issues related to race, inclusion, discrimination, or opportunity.* You can appoint a superbly qualified person to the CDO role, but they are not superhuman. That person can shepherd and steer a strategy, but that strategy must be owned by everyone.

What is problematic about DEI right now is that a lot of companies still think if they hire an extraordinarily talented CDO and give them real power, a sizable budget, and a team, they can rest assured that they have solved the DEI challenges in the company now and in the future. That is simply unrealistic and an unnecessary burden to put on even one function. That is an impossible ask of even the most heroically talented chief diversity officers. DEI is everyone's responsibility. A simple way of doing that is making DEI part of the goals of every employee in every function and requiring every business unit to have a function- or business-specific DEI goal.

For the most progressive companies and organizations, they are moving far beyond diversity, equity, and inclusion and they are embracing anti-racism. Because what happens in society and in organizations is that a lot of white people will say, "Well, I don't call anybody the *n*-word, I mentor people of color, and I have a Black person on my team who has been promoted. I'm not part of the problem." And without going too deep into anti-racism, what anti-racism suggests is that there are things you have to do to untie the knot of racism. It is not okay to just say, "I didn't do anything racist at my company." Anti-racism means that each person in the organization has to look around and see the knots of racism around the company and try to untie them. As the brilliant writer Isabel Wilkerson has analogized in her book *Caste: The Origins of Our Discontents*, racism in America is like a house we have all inherited. We may not have built it, but all the leaks and creaks are ours now, and each of us has a responsibility to fix it, just not the folks living in the small, dark, and damp places.

When you hear a company or organization announce that it has an anti-racism strategy, that is a high bar. Because diversity says that you will recruit people to the organization who are not all white. Equity says let's treat everybody fairly, which is a higher burden than diversity. Inclusion says, let's create an organization where no one feels like an outsider, where everyone feels like they are included in our processes, our programs, and our decision-making to the extent that they can. Belonging says, let's create an organization where anybody from any background can interview with us and come work here and feel like they can bring their authentic selves to this organization. Anti-racism is the highest bar because it requires everyone to identify and untie the knots of racism that exist in the organization. For more on anti-racism, please check out Ibram X. Kendi's excellent and groundbreaking book, *How to Be an Antiracist*.

While the CDO function has evolved to the point of analyzing and shepherding powerful strategies like anti-racism and other leading-edge DEI principles through the organization, it is still problematic to think that a single executive leader can advocate for and solve every DEI challenge. There is important infrastructure and there are powerful incentives organizations can implement to make sure that DEI is everyone's responsibility.

STOP HAVING THE CDO REPORT TO THE HEAD OF HR

Many companies struggle on the diversity front and part of that struggle stems from the structure of the chief diversity officer role. As I mentioned earlier, a big mistake is to have the DEI strategy embedded within one person as opposed to making it a company-wide responsibility. Diversity should be the responsibility of the entire employee population where people are held accountable and measured on that. It is not a cultural value if it is just Deborah, the CDO, who holds that value and Deborah is also the driver of the strategy and all the initiatives around DEI. That is not going to work if one person is responsible for everything.

The second thing that companies do that is largely problematic is they have the CDO report to the head of HR. Now, let me say at the outset that sometimes the CDO succeeds despite that reporting structure, but that is not the optimal ongoing reporting structure because the diversity function goes beyond human resources. It impacts supply chain, philanthropic partners, government relations, crisis management and communications, and many other functions and processes. If, as we learned in so many cases in the aftermath of George Floyd's murder, your CDO has to go through the head of HR to get to the CEO, that is too much bureaucracy in a real-time crisis to solve a mission-critical problem with internal or external stakeholders. As one CDO told me: "If I have to filter everything through the CHRO, I often lose the intensity and urgency of what I need to be successful."

The other problem in having the CDO report to the head of HR is that a lot of times the head of HR does not know a lot about diversity. They may know a lot about recruiting, or a lot about how to be a great HR business partner. They may have been a former total rewards executive or may have a learning and development background. All these sub-functions—talent acquisition, HR business partner, learning and development, total rewards—are areas an HR leader may have passed through at some point in their career and where they might have picked up relevant, core competencies in order to be an effective future CHRO. But many times, an HR leader does not have a lot of relevant, intensive experience in diversity. And so how can you manage, how can you measure, how can you mentor someone when you do not have the content expertise?

You do not know what is great or good or superlative in that function because you have never actually been involved in it. This, of course, is not true for every CHRO, but it is true for many, and these executives are often painfully unaware of their lack of expertise in DEI.

Early in my career, I interviewed for a chief diversity officer position at a company. I asked a mentor, a former CDO at a Fortune 50 company, for advice about the role. I expressed some skepticism about the role reporting into the head of HR and how, during my initial interview with the head of HR, I found her content expertise on DEI to be lacking. My mentor warned me that the reporting relationship and her lack of content expertise would ultimately undermine my ability to do my job well. She told me that all of the successes in the function would accrue to her, and all of the failures to me. She warned me that when it all hit the fan, and there was a racism crisis, it would be I, as CDO, who would shoulder the burden of fixing it in real time (as if that were even possible). I am not saying that is the case in all scenarios where a CDO reports to the head of HR, but there is a well-worn path of CDOs leaving organizations after one or two years because reporting into the head of HR did not set the CDO or the function up for success.

When a crisis hits, you realize you need somebody who has a direct line to the CEO to provide strategic counsel on the matter because the typical HR leader, though talented in many areas, can be quite unaware of the nuances of DEI. When George Floyd was murdered, a lot of organizations went through all this upheaval where the CEO had to make a statement, they had to do a series of town hall meetings, they had to refresh their diversity strategy, and many CEOs and senior HR leaders struggled in these moments. They had to do a whole new round of partnerships because the CEO promised, "Hey, we're going to give a hundred million dollars to Black charities to improve Black communities." The head of HR sometimes did not know what to do in any of those areas. They did not have crisis communications experience. They did not know what organizations to give money to and they were bereft of the skills required in this new post–George Floyd environment. And what we are seeing now is companies merging the diversity officer function with the head of human resources function and really putting a strong emphasis on their head of HR having a high level of intensive, through-the-fire diversity, equity, and inclusion experience.

Another reason to have the CDO report to the CEO and not the head of HR is that the chief diversity officer position is an absolutely strategic role. The CDO has enterprise-wide responsibility, just like finance, sales, marketing, legal, or any other enterprise-wide department. If a company has diversity, equity, and inclusion as enterprise-wide values, it has substantial opportunity and risk if they are done well or done wrongly or not done at all. You need an executive who has the ear of the CEO and has peer relationships with other functional leaders because there is a good chance DEI is going to have to collaborate with those executives on at least a weekly basis. If you are looking at launching into a new market and your marketing leader is rolling out a new strategy, wouldn't you want to ensure the marketing strategy covers the whole market? Don't you want to connect with the marketing leader to find out what the data says about the consumer appetites of African Americans, Hispanic/Latine, or women about your product? The CDO can be a great resource for you to identify which outside consultants you ought to work with or provide insights to help you launch that new product strategy. If you are doing a massive series of layoffs and your general counsel is concerned about whether or not the layoffs have impacted people of color disproportionately, who is in the best position to talk about that? Or if your company is facing a major regulatory or legislative change that will significantly impact its bottom line, and it turns out that Hispanic/Latine and Black legislators in Congress control relevant committee chairmanships, wouldn't you want your CDO, who may have relationships with those members of Congress, to be in the room when these policies are discussed? For these and many other reasons, the CDO should report to the CEO.

Despite my firm beliefs about this, I do think it is okay for the CDO to report to the head of HR in its inaugural framework. It is okay for three reasons. First, many companies do not fully understand how the CDO will operate in the culture in its inaugural format. Placing the CDO under the CHRO makes sense, especially if the HR leader is a culture carrier and has deep historical insight into the company or organization. Second, sometimes the biggest area of change needed is within the people function. Maybe the company needs to fundamentally change its culture or significantly improve its employee engagement with professionals of color. And third, many times CEOs do not want to add another direct report to their team and all new functions have to find another reporting structure. I still maintain, however, that once the DEI strategy solves some big problems and gets some momentum, it should be apparent to senior leaders that DEI is bigger than HR and is an enterprise-wide strategy. For that reason, it is okay to have the CDO report to the head of HR in its inaugural and initial framework. Within a short period of time (within two or three years), the CDO should report to the CEO.

Once you make that structural change and have your CDO report to the CEO, you will have to provide an actual budget. One of the of things that companies get wrong is that they do not set a budget. The CEO will many times generically commit to funding the role and will make promises to provide whatever resources are needed over time. That is great to say when you launch this new position. It becomes a whole different story once the CDO has been in place and he or she is fighting for scarce human and financial resources to manage this function. Often those promises are diluted or forgotten. The CDO supposedly runs a strategy that has enterprise-wide implications, and when we ask our clients what the budget is for the role, some respond that they have not really defined a specific budget. Companies can specify to the dollar what the marketing budget is. They can cite with great clarity and insight what the communications budget is. But the budget for the CDO is a great corporate mystery that no one can solve? The CDO should have a defined budget and allocated headcount just like their peers in the C-suite. Budgets and headcount are the lifeblood of functional effectiveness in complex organizations and the CDO should be given the same consideration as their executive peers.

The organization should commit to that up front, not say, "Well, we'll hire the CDO and they can figure it out." The company would not hire a general counsel as an individual contributor, you would not hire a CFO as an individual contributor, and you should not hire a CDO as a single contributor and provide two administrative staff reporting up to them and no budget at the outset of the hiring. Set an overarching budget, provide clarity on the headcount, and give your CDO flexibility after they come on board to figure out what the *specific* budget needs to be after a year in the seat. Give them the flexibility to figure that out and commit to funding the programs of the function, as well as the necessary headcount.

SEARCHING FOR YOUR NEXT CHIEF DIVERSITY OFFICER

In searching for your next chief diversity officer, it is important to understand that the role has changed significantly during the post–George Floyd era. Here are the competencies I believe are required for a CDO to succeed in a modern corporation or complex nonprofit organization.

A business strategist. Business and diversity strategies are inextricably linked, so your next CDO needs to understand the business landscape in your industry, disruptive threats from digital start-ups, and how to drive strategic change in your unique organizational culture. They will have to leverage innovation from diverse employees, source diverse vendor relationships, advocate policy with diverse governmental and regulatory leaders, and translate those elements into the overall enterprise strategy. Your next CDO needs the same strategic outlook and business acumen of your CFO, CIO, and CMO.

A patient influencer. The CDO needs to have the clarity and persuasiveness of your head of communications, the creativity of your chief marketing officer, and the ability to connect with diverse stakeholders like a big city mayor. In short, they need to have a deep understanding of the business, extraordinary communication skills, and keen emotional intelligence. Most importantly, they need to understand that the road to sustainable DEI is a long one.

A nimble pragmatist. Realistically, a company's diversity strategy can change, slow down, or come to a halt with new CEOs, new disruptions, a PR crisis, or numerous other challenges. Your CDO must be able to match the expectations of diverse stakeholders with the realities of the current organizational culture and opportunistically pounce when conditions are ripe for culture change.

A creative project manager. A new CDO might launch a new leadership program for diverse high potentials, develop a bonus incentive for senior leaders to hire and develop diverse talent, roll out that new supplier diversity platform, or other initiatives. And to do any of those successfully, they will need to galvanize buy-in with their small budgets, limited headcount, and pockets of organizational indifference. That takes creativity.

A number cruncher familiar with interpreting big data. A CDO needs to source, organize, retrieve, and analyze relevant diversity data and make sense of it for senior leaders. They will have to build collaborative relationships with functional leaders in audit, compliance, procurement, or IT, and to do that they need to understand the language of numbers and data.

A calming, strategic presence during PR crises. Let's hope that an executive at your company never sends a racist email, that your brand is not promoted inadvertently by the alt-right, or that a discrimination lawsuit at your company does not make front-page news, but chances are your company will experience a diversity crisis at some point. A CDO will help advise CEOs and senior management on *when* to respond to a public crisis, *how* to craft effective communications, and *which* diverse stakeholders to strategically engage.

A true believer with grit. Unlike a lot of roles in the C-suite, the chief diversity officer must see their work as a professional calling, as a commitment to social responsibility and making a difference in people's lives, because they are shepherding ideas and initiatives that go against the grain of most corporate cultures. Yes, they need strategic, technical, and communication skills but above all, they need old-fashioned grit to overcome inertia.

These seven leadership competencies speak to what a truly impactful CDO looks like. But there is one other requirement, and it is not a skill but a mindset. In our CDO searches, one thing we look for is what I call "diversity fatigue." That is a phrase I use to talk about the candidate pool of this function, because sometimes you get a chief diversity officer candidate who is on their third or fourth CDO role, and they are just worn down by all of the influencing, problem-solving, and crises. You do all of that three times and sometimes you just get burned out. And when they show up to their fourth CDO role, they think they have a tried-and-true template that can be applied with certain success. They don't bring a fresh look to the role and organization. I don't fault these executives at all because they have one of the hardest jobs in the entire company. At some point, diversity officers should maybe work for one or two companies and then they should move into consulting because they have such wisdom and trial-by-fire insight that they could help an entire industry of clients with information and resources and strategy about how to optimize their diversity initiatives. But to do a third or fourth CDO role in different organizations with measurable success one after another is very difficult and very rare. And so we sometimes look to see, does the person still have that fire in the belly the way they did with their first chief diversity officer role? My career advice to CDOs who start to feel burnout is to take a break from corporate CDO roles and go into DEI consulting or write and lecture on DEI as a thought leader. These executives have tremendous content expertise and can be very valuable to organizations in an early phase of DEI adoption. The silver lining of consulting and writing is that you do not get burned out by the work. You are not personally bearing the brunt of working within a possibly toxic or apathetic culture while you are trying to change it as a CDO.

THE FUTURE OF THE CHIEF DIVERSITY OFFICER ROLE

Today's CDO is a highly evolved, modernized executive as compared to the 1980s when the role first emerged. Back then, a lot of companies took their longest tenured person of color, created a new role for them called the Diversity Officer, and hoped for the best. This person was a great culture carrier, and they were well-known and largely trusted by the organization. They may or may not have had actual functional experience in the emerging professional function of diversity. In the 1980s and 1990s, the qualifications and background of the CDO was someone who came from human resources, or they were an employment lawyer, or were in government affairs and then moved into diversity.

Now we are seeing people coming into the CDO role from the business side, bringing incredible insight into how the actual company makes money, how it functions across global business and functional units, where the bottlenecks are. And they likely have experienced and benefited from some of the diversity initiatives the company has put forth, perhaps for high-potential talent, and they may have been mentored, sponsored, and developed for a leadership role. Our firm, Protégé Search, has even placed executives in the COO function who also had enterprise-wide responsibility for centering equity in the organization's work, processes, and partnerships.

I think that as long as companies listen to the views of the professionals and staff of color and heed the advice of their CDO and the team that reports into them, there is reason for optimism that this function can help transform companies and organizations for the better. If, however, CDOs remain stewards of an underfunded, underresourced, and unrealistic agenda that waxes and wanes according to the whims of executive leadership, these leaders will underutilize an amazing quiver of leadership competencies that never meet their mark.

CHAPTER FOUR

STOP DOING THIS: Having a Static DEI Strategy (or How the Murder of George Floyd Changed DEI Forever)

The last three years have been the most consequential in a generation for human capital and DEI leaders. There are moments in history that define a generation, moments that are so consequential that they impact people and society long after their occurrence. For example, Hurricane Katrina (2005), the terrorist attacks on the World Trade Center (2001), the fall of the Berlin Wall (1989), the first person on the moon (1969), and President Kennedy's assassination (1963) all made a deep and lasting impact on societies, even if you were born after any of those events took place. The murder of George Floyd (2020) was another consequential moment, and like most of the others, George Floyd had a profound impact on society and on business. If you are looking for diverse talent, the impact of George Floyd is part of the socio-psychological landscape for professionals of color; it shapes how POC think about corporate America, shapes their choices, and impacts their engagement and participation in the labor market. To put it simply, the collective reaction to George Floyd's murder changed the way DEI was structured and implemented, perhaps forever. **The big takeaway is that one thing companies must stop doing is thinking that their DEI strategy, once established, is set in stone.** If nothing else, the response to George Floyd's murder strongly suggests that having a living, flexible DEI strategy that can shape-shift with the dynamic movements of the twenty-first century is now a best practice in organizational design.

BLACK TRAUMA, WHITE DISCOMFORT, AND THE CIVIL RIGHTS CASE FOR DEI

For many companies and organizations, Floyd's murder created a once-in-a-generation inflection point on DEI. But I would like to offer the vantage point from professionals of color who are working at your companies and organizations. Because if hiring managers can understand the psyche of their diverse talent during this critical juncture in history, it is likely going to manifest in the establishment of a sustainable DEI strategy, not one that waxes and wanes with the news. It is critical for companies seeking diverse talent to understand how POC are thinking about politics, business, and their careers post–George Floyd, because if you think that people just leave their emotions at home and put on their game-day face when they show up to the office, you are mistaken. And you have to acknowledge that events outside of your company, tragedies and moments that happen in society, are going to take a significant toll on employee productivity. If you are a hiring manager, or a department leader, or running a section of a firm, or you are a CEO, it is naive to think that world events don't impact people. News like the Buffalo shooting at a supermarket (2022), or a church shooting in South Carolina (2015), or a shooting at a gay nightclub in Orlando (2016), or any other tragic event, when they happen, they impact employees.

One reason George Floyd's murder made such an impact globally was the visceral visual impact of it all. First of all, his murder was captured on video, and it was a white police officer, literally with his knee on the neck of a Black man while the Black man screamed for mercy. The white police officer who struck the killer blow was so indifferent to George's suffering, that he put his hands in his pocket while Floyd begged for his life and called out for his mother. Is there any human gesture more apathetic to human suffering than putting your hands in your pockets while another human gasps his last breaths? Meanwhile, the officer's whole face had a look of "I'm doing this, and what are you going to do about it?" as if he was proudly and arrogantly aware that he was being filmed. And the symbolism of white violence against Black people and the life being snuffed out as the man desperately calls for his mother—and nobody being able to stop this or intervene in anyway—the whole thing was emblematic of life in America for millions of Black people. Other deaths at the hands of police—Michael Brown, Freddie Gray, Breonna Taylor—all of them were horrific and exposed dark aspects of American society. But George Floyd was so symptomatic and emblematic of Black life in America for the last 400 years that it struck a unique and profound chord.

As a professional of color, you put this tragic scenario in the context of your career and life and it has an awkward resonance. Maybe you are working in a toxic work environment and maybe nobody cares. Maybe you are working underneath an abusive boss and everyone knows it, but ignores it. Maybe you literally get stopped by the police on occasion to and from work for no apparent reason and maybe the police officers have been aggressive and abusive toward you. Black people began to connect the violent white indifference to George Floyd's life to the apathy and, many times, abuse they experienced in their careers. White supervisors ignored their suffering and sometimes eagerly participated (even if behind the scenes) in their professional demise. That is not to make light of the fact that a Black man was murdered in cold blood and in broad daylight. But the relevance and symbolism of white indifference to Black suffering was a literal and figurative tragedy for Black people.

Let me give you an example of this. Several years before George Floyd's death, I was working at a leading public affairs firm as the co-head of the diversity practice when Alton Sterling was murdered. This was in 2016, and Alton's death followed a string of murders and beatings by white police officers. Many in the Black community were sad, mad, and marching in the streets. I called two of my three protégés who were African American men in their late twenties or early thirties, and asked, "How are you doing?" And they said, "Not well. Thank you for asking." And when I asked them how these events had impacted their work they responded that it had been very, very difficult to focus on work. Can you blame them? With Alton Sterling's murder by the police, with Philando Castile's murder, and a long line of murders by law enforcement officers, the news felt tragic and triggering. I invited them to lunch, and they talked about the range of emotions they were dealing with: anger, fear, resignation. They were not mad at their employer, and, in fact, they were working for a progressive company that gave them time and space to deal with this trauma. But still, the latest development between people of color and the police impacted them in a very emotional way.

Companies are now finally, I think, approaching mental health and wellness with a relevant, modern, and employee-centered approach. There really has not been as big of a focus on mental health and wellness as part of a total rewards strategy in previous eras of organizational life. Thankfully, we are now seeing companies really lean into mental health and wellness and connecting public affairs events in the news with what is happening with the mental state of their employees.

For a lot of organizations, their first response in the aftermath of George Floyd's murder was to hold a town hall meeting. And when executive leaders went in and heard what professionals of color were saying, many of the senior executives were surprised. Fellow employees of color were not surprised by what was said because it is what POC employees talk about among themselves. What they shared at these town hall meetings was that they are constantly under emotional stress in their organizations. People of color get few indicators that employers care about them personally or that the leadership of the organization cares about the issues that are important to them. On top of that, employees of color witnessed a wholesale lack of trauma by a good percentage of their white colleagues when these tragic news events happened. Few white employees think that driving to and from work might be a life-and-death scenario for them.

I have my own story that could have gone the way of George Floyd. I was working as a lawyer on Capitol Hill and I lived on Capitol Hill, but didn't have a car so I walked to work. One night, I went to Union Station to see a movie; it was the late show that got out at 1:00 a.m. My apartment was in a gentrifying neighborhood in Northeast Washington, DC. We lived right on the edge of a neighborhood where there had been a lot of crime. At the time, I was wearing what I typically wear now, which is preppy clothes: J.Crew shoes, J.Crew jeans, Ralph Lauren tortoise shell glasses, and a Harvard Law School sweatshirt. As I turned onto the street where I lived, a patrol car rolled up alongside me and a police officer asked, "Why are you running?" and I responded, "I'm trying to get back home; this is a bad neighborhood." And he then asked me to stop running, which I did, and then two other patrol cars showed up.

Now I am facing six police officers, two of them with guns drawn. Pretty soon I was on the hood of the police car with a gun pointed at my head and asked again, "Why are you running? Why are you running?" and I gave them the same answer as before: "I'm running because it's a bad neighborhood and I'm trying to get home. Look, my ID is in my pocket—I'm a lawyer for a member of Congress. Please look at my ID." And after figuring out who I was, they took their guns away from my head. As the officers were walking to their cars, I asked them: "Who did you think I was?" One of the officers replied: "The 'Capitol Hill Slasher,'" who reportedly was identified as Hispanic in the news. There had been a serial killer who was following pizza delivery drivers and robbing and shooting sometimes the driver and the homeowner who ordered the pizza. Disgruntled, I replied: "Really? Did he go to Harvard Law School?" (That could have been enough to get me killed.) Unfortunately, I know dozens of Black and Hispanic/Latino men who have a story like mine where they have been wrongfully accused and mistreated by law enforcement.

For many of us who are people of color, work is the sphere that brackets our personal lives and these moments of getting to and from work, or of enjoying ourselves during the weekend, these routine moments, like walking home from work, are sometimes fraught with fear, but almost always handled with some kind of emotional vigilance. And it is impossible to contain the stress and anxiety to the weekend or to our time away from work. That Monday I had to go to our weekly staff meeting with the congressman and analyze and discuss his votes on upcoming criminal justice, civil rights, and other legislation as if nothing happened. Was I likely less effective than I otherwise could have been? Most certainly.

That story reminds me that the lived experiences of employees who sit next to each other at work, who may be on the same Slack channel communicating about work projects, or who may take the same subway home together might still be vastly different after work and on the weekends. I was merely jogging home at 1:00 a.m.—that's it—and I was placed on the hood of a police car with a gun pointed at my head. How many white women have that story? How many white women, wearing their Smith or Bryn Mawr sweatshirt out jogging, have the police pull up to them and suspect them to be a serial killer and put a gun against their head? It just doesn't happen or, if it does, it is extremely rare. Yet, every Black man I know has been stopped by the police and many have been stopped multiple times.

This acknowledgment of the lived reality with your employee population is hugely important. I recently was hired by a large corporation to moderate several DEI sessions that were promoted internally at the company as "Critical Conversations on Race." The audience for these conversations was the executive leadership team and members of the board of directors. After two sessions, a Black board member delivered feedback from a white member of the board of directors. I was told that when I mentioned Donald Trump, the board member simply shut down and could not follow the rest of the discussion. I said to the person providing me the feedback, "I'm curious what I said about Trump that made him stop listening?" The Black board member replied: "It was just that you brought up Trump and injected politics into the conversation." I found that response curious and misguided. In a remark between questions to the panelists, I had simply highlighted the fact that majority white executive leadership teams and boards should be sensitive to the fact that there was consistent racist rhetoric coming from Trump and that almost certainly created an additional layer of stress for employees of color. That it was vital to understand that this rhetoric, plus the disproportionate impact of Covid on communities of color, profoundly impacted the workplace morale of employees of color.

I asked the board member and the other senior leaders from the company on the call if anything I was saying was not factually accurate. They did not dispute the facts. I essentially was being advised to not create discomfort for my audience. There could be no discomfort for white leaders even during sessions called "Critical Conversations on Race." I wound up firing that client. (My exact words were: "I don't think I'm the right consultant for your company; I'm a truth teller on DEI, and it sounds like you all don't want to hear the truth.") My fee of $15,000 per session was not worth being disingenuous on a topic as important as this one.

As a society, we have to acknowledge that this journey we are on to create a fair and equitable workplace will make some people uncomfortable, and that white discomfort is more than enough of a price to pay for equality. We're not asking for white people to be subject to the exclusion and unfairness that employees of color have experienced for decades. And we are not asking for white discomfort forever. We in the DEI community, practitioners and rank-and-file employees alike, are asking for our white colleagues to listen to our experiences. We are asking them to join us in asking and answering critical and difficult questions about caste systems in our organizations, about issues of equity, exclusion, and belonging. And yes, the questions and answers in this case might make white people uncomfortable.

The bitter and tragic irony is that people of color experience real challenges in the workplace and real trauma inside and outside of it. Yet, we now have a trend with Republican governors to demonize the truthful and accurate teaching of American history. These attacks on Critical Race Theory and DEI programs at universities and government institutions are nothing more than a ridiculous attempt at protecting white comfort. I get it: it must be difficult to hear about slavery, lynching, and systemic racism. *Imagine how difficult it must be to have actually endured slavery, lynching, and systemic racism?* White discomfort when hearing the truth is a small price to pay to ensure that that level of trauma never happens again.

I want to be crystal clear here. I am emphatically not saying that every white person in corporate America is racist. I am saying there are systems and structures that continuously create outcomes that reflect bias. For the overwhelming majority of companies in America and 99% of the companies and organizations we work with, the demographic makeup of the organization is eerily consistent. The management team is mostly white and male and the board of directors is mostly white and male. Middle management has more diversity, and the entry-level layer has the most diversity.

Why is that consistent across hundreds and thousands of companies and organizations? Because power and compensation are the most significant at the top of the organization and the beneficiaries of both have traditionally been white men. And if that is still true in 2023 just like it was true in 1973, that is not an accident. There are systems in place that produce that output and if you do not change those systems—even if you change the people, or the products, or the services, or the market, or your location—nothing will change.

What George Floyd's murder also revealed that a lot of people in corporate America do not talk about is that arguably the most significant inflection point in DEI happened because of civil unrest. For the past 30 years, the conventional wisdom was that the primary driver of DEI was the business case for diversity. The civil unrest, catalyzed by the Black Lives Matter protests that followed Floyd's murder, provided a mirror for Americans to take an unvarnished view of racism in the country. Businesses enacted bold and significant DEI programs and processes as a result. And perhaps, in some cases, the commercial outcomes supporting DEI, such as increased innovation, expanded access to customer markets, and improved employee retention and engagement, might have all of a sudden been so compelling that companies and organizations adopted more progressive policies and programs associated with DEI. But I am guessing the overwhelming majority of companies and organizations decided that DEI was about basic fairness in the workplace and in society. That there were tragic and problematic burdens unequally assigned based on the imaginary construct of race and that it would take significant, concerted, and sustained effort to eradicate those inequities.

And if that is true, then it means that grassroots leaders and rank-and-file employees may have successfully wrested the narrative about DEI from corporate leadership. That DEI is both about commercial outcomes *and* about fairness. That there is a business case for diversity *and* a civil rights case for diversity. That the lived experiences of people who work at a company or an organization are as important as the commercial or organizational outcomes. That philosophical shift might be the most enduring legacy for DEI in the aftermath of George Floyd's tragic and unnecessary murder.

CHAPTER FIVE

STOP DOING THIS: Focusing Too Much on Culture Fit in Recruiting

Another philosophy that companies have to abandon is putting too much emphasis on culture fit in hiring decisions. Culture fit is a powerful rallying cry for hiring managers. It is a way of ensuring new hires do things the way that existing professionals do within the organization. A company could be highly data-driven and make no decisions without first gathering and analyzing a considerable amount of data. Another organization might be consensus-driven and only make important decisions if a sufficient number of need-to-know executives have rendered their opinion on the matter. Another organization might have a command-and-control culture where hierarchy is deeply respected, while another might have a veto culture where someone from outside a business unit or function can opine on a new process or product without penalty.

When we recruit for companies, sometimes I find companies nervous about discussing culture fit. I think culture fit is a reasonable, if incomplete, framework for predicting success, but I also think it is a shortsighted and unrealistic notion to overrely on culture fit. The goal of DEI is to bring people from diverse backgrounds who have innovative ideas, new relationships, and different vantage points to solve problems and advance the organization's mission. Adapting to the dress code, the preferred technology platforms, and communication modes of the company is to be expected. What companies do wrong is that they use culture fit as a weapon of exclusion against professionals of color. Not fitting into the culture should be a source of productive tension at companies, not a reason to fire someone. And most times, it is the superficial elements of culture fit that are used to stymie the career development and the recruiting of professionals of color.

People of color have similar aspirations and motivations to the dominant white culture. They want to be paid fairly. They want as much responsibility as their professional capacities can handle. They want opportunities to demonstrate their leadership skills. But despite being motivated like everyone else, despite aspiring to the same things, they often struggle more than their white counterparts with the nuances of corporate culture, which is basically an extension of white, late-stage capitalist culture. What is asked of incoming people of color talent is, you may have your own culture where you come from but you need to adapt fully to us.

For example, at one company where I worked the new-hire orientation was called "Assimilation," and it was a week-long program where you got to meet the other new hires, learn about the company history, its approach to the market, core values, and other things. After that week-long Assimilation program I went to our offsite at the then-named Ritz Carlton Reynolds Plantation. After my 90 days, my white male boss, who was 65, said to me: "It seems like you're doing well, like you're enjoying yourself; how's it been so far?" And I said, "You know, it's been great; everyone is really nice, and I'm on some great projects. Once I showed up to Assimilation and then I went to the plantation, everything's been working out great." He responded, "That sounds awful!" It then dawned on him that, coming from a Black man, the names of those workplace events came across as awkward in the least and perhaps, upon deeper reflection, ridiculous.

And the reason it sounds awful is because the sequence of those programs and their names sound like slavery. Black people went to the slave block, were assimilated into the life on the plantation, and then went to work on the plantation. And it did not bother my white male boss that our offsite was at a plantation; he hardly gave it any thought. But what would a German do if Mercedes-Benz said to their German workforce, "Hey, our orientation's going to be at the concentration camp." Would any German find that acceptable? Would they go along with that? But a white southerner found it completely okay to host and select a place with *plantation* in the name. What's more, the entire senior management team at a company apparently signed off on calling employee orientation Assimilation for a decade or more.

New-hire orientation is rarely called assimilation anymore, but the dynamics of it are the same. It is a process to help people adhere to the "way things are done" at any particular company or organization. Assimilation is the opposite of the core principles of DEI because assimilation says whatever makes you unique and distinctive, we want to deemphasize that. Instead, we want you to meld into the overall persona and ethos of who is already here. It is the whole melting pot notion that is a failed cultural idea from a hundred years ago. It has no credibility in modern society, but companies are essentially assimilating people to their "culture." Orientation is a way of doing that, a way of cycling everybody through the same process to hopefully create a refined company man.

There is a generational shift that has to happen with Baby Boomers in particular, who sometimes have this notion of cranking out the company man to learn the ideal and suitable company ways to fit in. I think most orientation programs primarily serve to help make leaders comfortable with new talent and only partially to help these new employees feel like they belong. In doing that, they are giving up out-of-the-box thinking, innovation, experimentation, and diverse points of view. It is understandable that everybody should learn to row in the same direction, but you can row in the same direction with a Black Lives Matter T-shirt on and a nose ring, the same way you can with a Patagonia vest or a custom suit. As long as your employees don't impede company progress, who cares how they look? They are rowing in the same direction. The problem is that companies think about rowing in the same direction as a way to control people, as if the mechanics of rowing are more important than the fact that everyone is rowing in the same direction. But by creating this company man that is homogeneous and assimilated into the company, the individualism that is ripe and rich with value disappears and is kept at bay and, as a result, companies never get the most value and impact out of their staff.

Cultural assimilation is one of the practices that prevents so many companies from getting the best productivity out of people who are not homogeneous, who are not part of the dominant culture. What could a company gain with a little bit of diversity? For starters, insight on new markets, access to new markets, and a better understanding of how people think—how consumers think in these new markets. That fresh-out-of-college Black kid you just hired is also a consumer, right? You can preview the colorway for an apparel line with Gen Z employees. You could ask an Indigenous ERG group if an advertising campaign reeks of cultural appropriation. You could preview a philanthropic partnership with an internal LGBTQ focus group before committing funds to it. And employees who are military veterans might have some keen insights into programming around Veterans Day and Memorial Day. If you do not have young people, people of color, people with varying physical abilities, the neurotypical and the neurodivergent weighing in on these and other decisions, then you could be making a huge mistake, waste a ton of money, squander goodwill, tarnish your brand, or worse—lose customers and employees.

What company only wants upper-class or white customers? Even luxury and exclusive brands, like Louis Vuitton, want a broad and diverse set of customers considering the fact that street wear, the style and fashion of urban, multicultural youth, is all the rage. So, what is Louis Vuitton doing? They are partnering with Black designers to figure out how to get Gen Z to wear Louis Vuitton clothing. They have hired hip-hop rapper and producer Pharrell Williams as men's creative director. So instead of enforcing a stodgy, inflexible, and melting pot culture, innovative companies and organizations are bringing arbiters of diverse culture into the fold and seeking to change their internal culture to make it more diverse and more disruptive in its thinking. In that way, these organizations are ensuring they do not become a Blockbuster Video in a Netflix world of multiculturalism.

If the data shows the senior leadership in most companies and organizations is white and male, then what does it predict about the culture of the organization? That it reflects the values, habits, and principles of white, affluent men. I think that some white people believe there is not a white culture; they think that there is simply culture, that there is just this natural organizational amniotic fluid we live in that is bias-free and neutral. But people of color can sense from even the recruiting process when culture feels like upper-middle-class white culture.

For example, during an interview with a company, I was asked the question, dead serious, as if I had surely been asked it before: "Where do you summer?" What is that? *Summer* as a verb. Hmm. I thought it was a season and a noun as a part of speech, but I experienced *summer* during that interview as a verb. If I had said, "Well, my cousin Keisha always does a big barbecue, and we go down to North Carolina, and I'm typically responsible for getting the liquor, so I always bring a case of Crown Royal . . ." what do you think would have happened? I think you know that I would have gotten an odd look, an uncomfortable silence, and a nervous clearing of the throat. That is because what the person who asks, "Where do you summer?" wants to hear is that I go to Martha's Vineyard, or the Hamptons, or to Newport, Rhode Island, or possibly the Outer Banks in North Carolina. Bonus points for the south of France, the Algarve in Portugal, or Costa del Sol in Spain. When I answer with the preferred destinations, I am now speaking a cultural language that makes me relevant. It signals that, "I'm one of you." That might come easy and natural to me, someone with a Harvard degree who "summered" in the Vineyard for 10 years, who travels to Europe, who watches French and Italian independent films, who otherwise enjoys many aspects of white affluent culture as well as urban Black culture.

Imagine a kid who is not only FGBT, but first-generation college, maybe from a small HBCU or state school, whose parents are blue collar, and you ask them such pointed and class-conscious questions in an interview. You might not get an answer you expect, and, most importantly, that answer may also be irrelevant to that person's performance in the role. It might not be what you would like to hear in your unconscious attempt to further homogenize your organization's culture, but it is almost certainly not related to the tasks and leadership competencies needed to succeed in the role.

I can imagine the thought bubble over your head: "But wait a minute, white professionals from disadvantaged backgrounds get hired all the time and they don't get the benefit of the doubt, either; so, this is a problem that everyone has to deal with." That is partially true. I had an officemate when I was a summer associate at a law firm who was Italian-American. We shared stories of feeling like an outsider in this prestigious law firm and shared tips on how to fit into the upper-middle-class culture at the firm. We became fast friends, and we remain friends to this day. Mike is now a very accomplished partner at one of the top law firms in the country. It is fair to say that he also had to run a gauntlet of fitting into a culture that was foreign to him, and apparently that burden did not hold him back, career-wise. I would argue that there are some benefits of the doubt afforded to my white friends like Mike that are not afforded me.

First, Mike's cultural deficiencies likely are going to begin and end with him, and not represent an entire race. Unlike a professional of color, Mike is not going to represent the entirety of his race if he doesn't fit in at the company. When he doesn't write an error-free memo, he is not writing on behalf of all Italian-American lawyers. Unfortunately, given the dearth of professionals of color working at elite companies and organizations, there is a tendency to associate the entire cultural traits of a race to the lone representative (or one of a few) who work at the enterprise. Think I am exaggerating? Have you ever seen someone who is white fail spectacularly at the job and then their boss or the CEO retort: "Well, that's the last time we hire another white guy." Yet, these conversations happen all the time when an "other"—a Black, Hispanic/Latine, LGBTQ, Indigenous, or Asian American—professional fails. Of course, it is never stated in public conversations, but it becomes almost an unspoken conspiracy among leaders associated with the next hire. Unfortunately, when a person of color fails in an important role at a company or organization, hiring managers tend to think twice about hiring another person of color to replace them. It is as if they think, "Well, we tried; let's get back to the usual way of doing things."

Second, any cultural deficiencies Mike might have likely are going to be smoothed out by his white mentor. He is likely going to hit the mentor lottery, whereas a Latina woman likely is going to lose out. And one thing a great mentor does is they help you understand the unspoken cultural nuances of working at an organization. They tell you who really has power and must be treated with deference despite their lack of title. They tell you which company events you have to show up to. They help you understand the moments when your irreverence will be rewarded and the ones where you will seem rude and uncouth. And most importantly, a great mentor will contextualize your mistakes when you get all this wrong. My friend Mike might show up in the firm's garage in a red Mustang because that was his dream car growing up on Long Island, but he will soon be told that he should drive an Audi, BMW, or Mercedes in some understated color if he wants to become partner.

And third, related to the mentoring issue, I have found it is very difficult for white senior managers to talk candidly to professionals of color about the soft and unspoken rules inside the organization. There was a young man I mentored at a high-profile company; he was in middle management hoping to get into senior management. I knew from conversations with other leaders in the organization that he was not taken seriously for a promotion to senior management because of the way he dressed and the way he spoke, which included a penchant for punctuating his sentences with urban slang. This young man was very valuable to the company—he had a savant-like quality that allowed him to understand the nuances of a particular segment of the business in more depth and complexity than anyone else in the organization. But he would come to work every day looking like he was going to a night-club. I was a mentor to him, so I asked him, "Hey, man, what's with the outfits?" He had a chain outside of his tie, he wore baggy slacks, square-toed shoes, everything was a tan color, and I asked, "Where are you going? You look like you're going to the club after work." And he said, "I've got to walk to the bus stop from my apartment complex with my neighborhood friends in the Bronx, and I don't want to be wearing a navy Brooks Brothers suit and tie because they'll think I've sold out. On the corner you would think that I'm just a regular guy off the block and we're just talking, shooting the breeze like we used to back in the day. And then I get on the bus and I'm working at this big company in the fancy Manhattan offices. But to my friends on the block, I'm just a kid from the 'hood. And I can't ever get too big that I forget them. So, how I dress is letting them know that I'm still the same guy they grew up with. It's more important for me to signal to them than it is to sig-nal to people here." And I responded, "Okay, I get it—that's fine. Why don't you bring a different jacket, different shoes, and keep them here at work? Just go from Clark Kent to Superman or Superman to Clark Kent. But you need to costume up because what you're signaling here is that you're not one of us, and the reason the company gives you a Jos A Bank and a Brooks Brothers employee discount is because they want you to wear traditional corporate clothes. That's why I dress the way I dress. Do you think I want to wear this tight-ass suit? You know I don't. I'd rather be in a hoodie and T-shirt and shorts, but that's not signaling that I'm a player in this game."

As an advisor on DEI, I was more successful in helping this young Black executive change his attire than I was in convincing the CEO that they should abandon the suit-and-tie requirements for employees. I personally thought that rule was outdated and stodgy, but I had not won that battle yet. In the meantime, I had to help this young Black man understand that by not adapting somewhat to this cultural cue, he was holding himself back professionally. I was at least relieved to know that he received an offer of employment despite the fact that he very likely dressed like that during his interview. I am guessing his incredible skill and talent shone through. My other point is that no white peer or supervisor ever mentioned his clothing choices to him once he joined the company. Maybe they did not know how to approach him with this advice. Maybe they did not notice his attire. Or maybe, they simply did not care enough to help him.

The price companies pay to foster and sustain white culture is something not talked about much. The old trope I have heard countless times about culture is the layover test: those on the interview team should measure the candidate's fit, in part, on how they would get along with that person if they were on a long layover at an airport. I have been in that exact scenario, and I bonded with my colleague in a way that I would not have if we were simply going to the client site, grabbing lunch, and then heading back to the hotel. And I have seen other professionals of color pretty much ignored because the white supervisor just assumed that they did not have anything in common with the Black or brown professional they were stuck in the airport with. I was lucky that my colleague and I found a conversational sympatico with men's fashion and found ourselves on the dusty conversational paths of sports debates and college hijinks. Many up-and-coming professionals of color are not so lucky. And, yes, it is also true that professionals of color have to get out of their comfort zones as well to forge these relationships. But white leaders abandoning their assumptions about culture fit based on a cursory glance at their colleagues of color would go a long way to creating a dynamic and elastic sense of culture where everyone is welcome, club suit or not.

Because so much of corporate culture is white affluent culture, it is just assumed that you, as a person of color, are comfortable with white people. You have to navigate the issue of trusting your colleagues, and for many people of color, this is the largest number of white people they have ever trusted in their life. If you live in America, you likely live in a largely segregated environment. Your neighborhood is probably not integrated; your church is not integrated; your social organizations, book clubs, hobbies, friends—even your social media groups—likely are not integrated. But you spend the most time in the day at the place where you are the starkest minority and you are expected to navigate that with ease.

For example, I had a Black executive I coached at a large company in the aerospace industry and this person was new to a marketing role. I spoke with the CEO and asked, "What are we hoping to solve for with the coaching?" The CEO responded that this Black male executive needed to be more creative, that he needed to take more risks. He was a communications executive, but now was in a hybrid marketing and communications role and needed to be more creative and innovative. I talked to the executive I was coaching to figure out what the barriers were to him taking more risks. The risks were not intellectual; they actually were rooted in his socioeconomic background. He said, "At this company, if you do a good job— not a *great* job—if you just do a good job and you don't die, you eventually become senior vice president. And that's where the big money happens. I'm not going to do anything right now that might jeopardize my path to senior vice president. And as a director, I have two levels to go." And then he continued, "In my entire family, I have the biggest, most lucrative job in the extended family. Everybody looks up to me and I provide for a lot of people in the family. The worst thing that could happen to me is for me to lose this good job, so I'm not taking any risks."

I went back to the CEO and said that it was not intellectual, it was not that the executive was incapable of doing the work, it was that he didn't want to take any risks and lose his job. I told him that if you want him to be more creative and take more risks, you will have to provide him some cover. He needs to know that he can trust you.

The other thing I learned in coaching this Black executive was that, as a person unfamiliar with marketing, he was not properly trained in marketing, and he was unprepared to excel in this new function. In marketing, failure is par for the course. Part of your job in marketing is to pitch a dozen ideas and maybe one or two of them will take root and turn into something, but 10 of them might fail. Nobody cares about the 10 that were crazy and failed. But that is not how a communications person thinks because everything they do has to be perfect—they have to bat 1.000. They are thinking that, to use the baseball metaphor, they cannot bat .330 or less. They are thinking, "I have to hit it out of the park each time." If the CEO can give him cover, if the CEO can have his back so he has the room to fail, he will take more risks. And that is exactly what happened. With my counsel, the CEO gave this executive a stretch assignment, promoting him to head of marketing at one of the plants in South Carolina. Despite some personal challenges, he had a great career at that company and was recruited a few years later to be the chief communications officer at a Fortune 20 company. The main issue for this spectacularly talented executive was not one of competence, it was really an issue of trust, and along with trust, the ability to take risks. That is not something you will see on a résumé, but it is lurking in the back of the mind of professionals of color all the time: Can I trust this company to back me up if I take a big risk and fail?

Culture fit is complicated. What can companies and organizations do to make sure professionals and executives stick and stay within their culture? The most important thing is to understand that culture should not always be set from the top; it can and is often set throughout the organization by its current managers and its new employees, despite what senior leaders may think or hope. Like any thriving city with vibrant neighborhoods, organizations have their own unique traditions and cultures in various areas. And like all great cities, organizations would do well to allow room for new people and the natives, for the wealthy and the strivers, to bring their own traditions to the rich and dynamic culture that you hope to create in your organization.

THE CULTURE OF THE CORPORATE TOURNAMENT

There is a fallacy, I believe, a misguided belief, that I think companies make far too often: not recognizing that this code-switching—the toggling back and forth between their own culture and the upper-middle-class white culture of corporate America—is exhausting for professionals of color. It is sometimes like walking around land mines. Or sometimes it is getting the answer wrong and suffering the awkward consequences. I once had a situation where we were at lunch outside the office and a colleague asked everybody who was the greatest drummer of all time. Of all time? Easy. Art Blakey, the jazz drummer. He looked at me like I was from another planet and asked, "Who is that?" I said, "Art Blakey is a jazz drummer." And the colleague shot back, "No, no, no. I'm talking about, you know, rock music." And I wanted to say to him, you said the greatest of all time—all time, all genres. I could have responded DJ Marley Marl, who never used a drum set, but used a drum machine. Instead, I was excluded from the conversation and the colleague went on to say maybe it was the guy from The Cure, or maybe the drummer from The Who. And I am sitting there, literally by myself, and all these other white people are coming up with drummers who are the "greatest of all time." I ate my burrito in silence, hoping the conversation would shift back to some mutually interesting topic, but it never did. I felt awkward, out of place, and embarrassed. I did not say anything offensive, but I somehow missed the cultural cue embedded in his question that everyone else picked up. I started learning to avoid chiming in on those conversations and just to listen and observe. Over a few years, I am sure I missed out on some moments to build social relationships with my colleagues, but the sting of being culturally off center was a constant reminder for me.

Even seemingly culturally ubiquitous topics can be awkward to navigate. In the 1990s, every Friday morning I was asked by my colleagues, "Did you see *Seinfeld* last night? Oh my God, it was crazy," and they just assumed that I watched *Seinfeld*, a show with no Black characters in it. Or they would ask me about *Friends,* another show with no Black characters, and I would respond that I watched *Living Single.* I would get the usual response, "What is that? I've never heard of it." I was like, "It's literally what *Friends* was based on. It's a bunch of Black folks who live together but instead of a waitress, chef, and actor, the *Living Single* characters are an attorney, stockbroker, and business owner." But few white people watched it because it was a Black TV show reflecting Black professional culture. And I was thinking that there is not a white character on *Living Single*, and there is not a Black character on *Friends*, but you expect me to watch *Friends*.

Even the water-cooler conversations that you will have in a company, the terms and the nuances of those conversations, are set according to white, upper-middle-class values and systems. If somebody asks me how my summer reading list is coming together and I respond that I am reading Malcolm Gladwell's book *David and Goliath* or Toni Morrison's canon, that signals that I am still Black, but I am reading mainstream books by authors white people have heard of. But if I say I am reading Raekwon's autobiography, *From Staircase to Stage,* about his transformation from drug addict to leader of Wu-Tang Clan and record label entrepreneur, my white colleagues probably have never heard of that and they would conclude that this guy reads weird stuff.

Even though code switching is exhausting, it is almost impossible as a leader of color to avoid it in most complex, majority-white organizations. It is especially important for people of color who want to compete in the corporate tournament to be well-versed in at least some aspects in white culture so they can make some personal connections with their white colleagues. Code switching can start as early as the interview process. For example, when we coach our executive candidates for a position, we ask them to tell us something about themselves personally so they can guide the conversation on their terms. For women of color, for example, they can talk about their hobbies, whether that is traveling, or running, or singing in their church's gospel choir—it doesn't matter, but it is important to have something in mind to build early rapport with them so our clients do not start with a blank slate. Because if the client asks them a crazy, irrelevant question like "Where do you summer?" the interview will go off the rails because the candidate will think, "Where did I summer? Did I answer that question right? What did they mean by that? I said I went to North Carolina to my family reunion, but I don't know if that was right. The interviewer looked startled when I said that."

The larger point is that white hiring managers have to come a little bit farther with people of color to meet in the middle, to not make the water-cooler conversations or the rapport building time all about white, European, affluent culture, which is what it often is. The rapport building or sidebar conversations that white hiring managers make with professionals and executives of color in interviews are almost never about Black or Indigenous or Hispanic/Latine culture. Is it fair that white hiring managers have to do more to build trust with POC candidates? No. It is also not fair that POC candidates have to learn to navigate two cultures just to even the playing field in the corporate tournament. There is much more to do to reduce or eliminate code switching within organizations, and starting at the interview process to make it as even of a playing field as possible is a great practice.

Consider a hypothetical situation where the roles, the environment, and the corporate culture are completely flipped: you are a white candidate and you go to interview for a job at a majority Black company. Your interview is in January, and you show up to the parking lot and all the cars have college stickers like Morehouse, Xavier, and Spelman, along with fraternity and sorority names like Alpha Phi Alpha, Alpha Kappa Alpha, Omega Psi Phi, Delta Sigma Theta, Kappa Alpha Psi, Phi Beta Sigma, Zeta Phi Beta, and so on. When you are signing in, a couple of people are joking around, and they ask you if you have seen the meme going around about the Black woman in the church making the fraternity and sorority founders' day announcements. You would have to know that almost all of the Black fraternities and sororities were founded in January, and you would have to know that, in the Black church, they celebrate all the birthdays each month by announcing who in the congregation was born that month. And so the joke is that because many of these Black fraternities and sororities were founded in January, we are going to treat it like we would in a Black church, and we are not even giving you a day to celebrate, you are just lumped in with all the other fraternities and sororities founded that month. If you are white, you are like, wait a minute. I don't get that. The fraternity and sorority is still active? You celebrate the founding day and it is a big deal? Yes, Black fraternities and sororities do not die when you leave college—they are lifelong memberships. I was initiated into my Black fraternity as an adult, when I was 34, for instance. So, Black fraternities and sororities still celebrate, they still have activities, they still have leadership, and they still play an important part in the lives of Black professionals far beyond the college years.

When you get to the interviewer's office, you notice that he has a picture of Reginald Lewis on the wall and he has an antique record player—you can see that he is a jazz and hip-hop fan. He starts the interview by saying, "Okay, I'm going to keep it simple. Who's the best, Notorious B.I.G. or Tupac, and why? You know that B.I.G. sold nearly 60 million records and Tupac over 75 million records so they're both successful, but who's the best, and why?" And after you have put together your answer, your interviewer has a different "easy" question. "What do you think the follow-up will be to the Year of the Return?" And what the interviewer is talking about, what they expect you to know, is that the Year of Return is Ghana inviting displaced Africans from the slave trade back to Ghana, welcoming them back home in 2019, 400 years after the slave trade started. And you are sitting there trying to cobble together some smart answers because you want the job. You went to the University of Oregon and now you are here interviewing at this Black company feeling like you are the outsider from the minute you walk up. What you are experiencing is exactly what most POC candidates experience. They have to navigate all the culture cues and underpinnings of white, affluent culture often from the very first moments of interviewing for a job at the company or organization.

If that anecdote was a head-spinning experience of cultural ignorance and awkwardness, you now have a good sense of what millions of professionals of color experience from their interviews to water-cooler conversations to company offsites: the challenge of fitting into a culture that is largely foreign to you, but necessary for you to understand if your career is to progress.

CHAPTER SIX

STOP DOING THIS: Allowing the Fake Failed Search to Thwart Your DEI Recruiting Strategy

The intention to be more diverse is step one in being able to adapt and thrive in a changing, competitive landscape. But no matter how deeply, how broadly, or how often you state that intention, without concrete steps to become more diverse, it is likely that you'll have a lot of turnover, and you will never get to a critical momentum. Recruiting diverse talent at scale is step two and I have seen several patterns emerge in how companies that intend to be more diverse actually have processes and biases in place that thwart those efforts. One such tension is the scenario where diversity executives and the HR executives are the evangelists for DEI in the workplace and they are trying to move a recalcitrant organization into a progressive direction. And they are meeting resistance primarily from white line managers and executives who respond, "I get it with DEI, but *I just want to hire the best person available.*" That's a highly biased comment because, if you were hiring the best person available, the organization would not be demographically skewed toward white people. It would not, unless you can prove that there's disproportionate qualification and genius in the white community versus other demographic groups. That is simply incorrect. Intelligence is equally distributed throughout the world, but for many organizations the first hurdle to overcome, through the seemingly benign comment of "I just want to hire the best person," is the self-fulfilling and largely unconscious mindset that because you are a largely white organization and you have positive commercial or organizational outcomes, it must be *because of the whiteness of the people who are there.* Not only does the success of your organization not hinge on the whiteness of your employees, your organization, like the PGA Tour and every sports league has learned, would almost assuredly be even more successful if you had more diversity, equity, and inclusion in the organization.

The diversity and HR leaders are pushing the line managers, functional leaders, and hiring managers, and those people tend to be white men. And what happens is, these DEI and HR managers will say, "Oh, and by the way,

105

we found a resource for you to use, a diversity recruiting firm." And now the line manager or the hiring manager is working with the diversity search firm. The white male hiring manager is not going to tell us, "Hey, Rory, you know what? I think all this diversity stuff is BS. I think you're BS. I believe in meritocracy and this DEI stuff flies in the face of everything I've ever done as a hiring manager." They're never going to say that. Instead, they'll say, "On today's call let's talk about Hank and Marsha and Keisha. None of them are right, and here's why." And they'll give the most ridiculous, slimmest, superficial of reasons why they are excluding the entire slate of people. They will require the candidate to meet 99% of the criteria when they, in fact, did not meet 99% of the criteria when they were hired. Yet Jamal and Keisha have to represent 99% of the criteria, so the bar becomes higher to offset the subtle, unconscious bias that the white hiring manager has. And on and on the search goes with no one who is seen as sufficiently qualified for the role. Soon the hiring manager is micromanaging every element of the search, almost guaranteeing that it is going to fail. It is the same as looking at the pomegranate and saying, "Well, I just want one that peels like an apple, but the way this pomegranate peels is different. The skin is too thick. I don't like it. I like cutting my fruit a certain way and get-ting to the core of it. And I can't eat the inner core of this thing the same way. So this pomegranate is not qualified as a fruit."

The hiring manager is also thinking, "We did just fine before this diversity initiative happened and, whatever biases I have, they didn't cre-ate any spectacular failures." And if the hiring manager did bring in or promote someone who was a spectacular failure, that person's failure will be uniquely attributable to them, not to their race or to a recruiting initia-tive. They will also critique the white candidates harshly because they are not stupid, they are not going to say only the Black candidates are bad because that would show an obvious bias. The hiring manager finds fault with everything with all the candidates, they suspend the search, and they fire the diversity search firm. Somebody gets blamed for the failure, typically the recruiting firm or the Black or POC recruiter, or the person trying to implement diversity. The internal diversity, talent, or HR executive gets reprimanded or fired. And then, of course, the hiring manager is compelled to take matters into their own hands and restarts the search with the same mantra: "I just want to hire the best person." And who do they typically find? They find an internal white candidate or someone in their network who is white. The whole scenario becomes this evergreen argument against the principle of diversity recruiting.

But what happens when a white candidate doesn't work out after an inclusive hiring process yields them as the placement? I remember a scenario in which I caught a white candidate lying about his compensation. I asked for his compensation expectations on four occasions (it is illegal to ask for a candidate's compensation in certain states). The candidate self-disclosed that he made $500,000, then $700,000, and then finally $900,000. He then adjusted the last figure to $950,000. I told my client that this was a serious red flag and that, for the first time in my recruiting career, I was recommending to a client that they not make a particular hire. The client hired the candidate anyway and dismissed my concerns because he personally knew the candidate's boss and he knew that individual wouldn't have recommended him if he lacked integrity.

My placement, an SVP at a consumer-focused company, was fired within the first six months. Want to guess what for? Yep: an overall lack of integrity and ethics. Do you think the company, my client, thought twice about hiring a white senior executive after that? Do you think they thought twice about the nominations they got from other white leaders in their network? I don't think so. I don't think there was any blowback about that candidate's whiteness and how they might approach recruiting white candidates. **Nor should there be.** That executive does not represent all white people. He only represents himself. He had the questionable ethics and integrity. I think, in many cases, however, there would be a different reaction if an executive of color did not work out in these same circumstances. Just like in the fake failed search scenario, the blowback would have been so significant that it would have impacted future candidates of color and maybe even current executives of color in that company (the question might be raised of how many unqualified candidates of color might have slipped through a shoddy recruiting process). Heck, the diversity recruiting firm might even get a "mixed" review about their recruiting efficacy ("mixed" is the kiss-of-death term for professionals of color). That would be wrong in all of those cases. DEI would take a quantum leap forward if candidates and executives from every background were afforded some of the grace that is sometimes liberally granted white executives and candidates.

My advice is to not let the fake failed search derail your diversity recruiting strategy. It is important to call out this scenario the moment you spot it, and that is usually when you hear the unfair and overly intensive scrutiny given to candidates of color on slates. The moment you sense that almost no one is good enough for the job is the moment to call out the potential fake failed search before everything goes downhill. It might not only save this particular search, but it might save your overall diversity recruiting strategy.

CHAPTER SEVEN

STOP DOING THIS: Believing Your Organization Is a True Meritocracy

The fake failed search is a symptom of a larger issue bedeviling many companies and organizations: the myth that they are a true meritocracy. I am a passionate believer that *systems* create the outcomes in organizations, companies, societies, and even nations. The systems within companies and organizations produce white men as their predominant leaders not because white men are more qualified than women and people of color, but because there are overt and subtle systems that further those outcomes. The under-leveling of professionals of color, the unequal bestowing of executive sponsorship, the divergent ways stretch assignments are doled out, the unequal pay and its associated motivations, the unfairness in performance reviews, the lack of transparency and inequity in the promotions process, sexual harassment and racial discrimination, and several other factors all conspire to create the unequal outcomes in corporate America.

The data about corporate leadership paints a damning picture within corporate America. According to a McKinsey & Company report, Black workers make up 12% of the entry-level workforce and just 7% of the middle and senior management. After middle management levels, the numbers begin to dip considerably: Black workers make up 5% of the workforce at the senior manager level. At the senior vice president level, 4%. Only 1% of Fortune 500 CEO spots are held by Black leaders. McKinsey & Company estimates that, if these statistics and trends continue, it could take nearly 100 years before Black employees reach parity in corporate America.[1]

Systems produce outcomes. I believe the same is true, for instance, in basketball and golf. Those sports leagues produce those vastly different racial outcomes—the NBA is over 70% Black, and the PGA Tour is over 60% white—because there are vastly different sets of infrastructure, from player camps and training programs, to available equipment, to available coaches and practice venues, to role models, that help produce those outcomes. White people are not predisposed to be great golfers and Black people are not predisposed to be great basketball players. Systemic forces and their myriad and associated impacts produce them.

The counterargument when I mention this at conferences or in professional conversations is to highlight the incredible competencies of the existing (white) leadership at Company X or Organization Y. I have never maintained that white executives in companies and organizations are not smart, hard-working, diligent, and highly ethical for the most part. I emphatically believe that Bill Gates is a brilliant entrepreneur, that Jack Welch was an incredible visionary, and that Jamie Dimon is an exceedingly astute CEO. I am equally emphatic in saying that there are likely dozens of people of color like these white men both inside of their companies and within their high school and college classes who could have produced the same professional outcomes if they had the same systems working in their favor. I believe Bobby Jones, the legendary golfer, was a gifted athlete. I am equally certain that there were Black golfers of equal talent—the Tiger Woodses of their day who were unknown within the white world—who would have helped reduce Jones's trophy count had they been given the same set of advantages and been allowed to compete. That is why the core of this book is about reforming talent systems so that the most talented professionals rise to the top, not the ones who have the privilege of better infrastructure to their benefit.

The other reaction I typically get is the argument about the lack of overt racism inside the company or organization. If there is no overt racism, then all of the outcomes must be merit-based, right? And by racism, people almost always mean specific, overt acts against an employee or employees of color. That is an incredibly oversimplistic way to measure inequality in an organization. The better way is to look at the outcomes. If no Black person in 15 years has ever made partner or made it to the senior vice president level, is that because Blacks are innately inferior? Of course not. It is because there are dozens of systems and processes at the macro, but mostly the micro level, that help produce those results. There is a plethora of research reports and books that analyze this issue in greater detail than I do in this book. David Thomas's *Breaking Through: The Making of Minority Executives in Corporate America* remains, in my opinion, the best first book or reference guide about the foundational principles of DEI, and what companies do to help advance leaders of color to the senior executive ranks. Michele Alexander's *The New Jim Crow: Mass Incarceration in the Age of Color Blindness* analyzes systemic forces creating vastly different outcomes in the criminal justice system, a relevant framework for how systemic inequality produces unfair outcomes by race. My point here is to get hiring managers and executive leaders to analyze critically the systems that produce the outcomes in their companies and organizations. The lazy and self-serving approach is to dismiss inequality as an organizational myth, when believing the enterprise is a true meritocracy is the real practice of mythmaking. I am not advocating that equal outcomes be mandated; I believe reforming systems holds the key.

As I noted, this inequality has many fathers. The under-leveling of professionals of color is one pernicious, systemic issue I too often see operationalized at companies. What I mean by under-leveling is the hiring of a candidate of color with similar credentials as a white candidate but at a lower rank and title than a white candidate. A big tech company tried to recruit me for a role as the head of global diversity recruiting. I was intrigued by the scale of the role and decided to take the interview. When I asked what the title and level of the role were, the recruiter first dismissed the question as irrelevant, but when I persisted, she noted it was a senior manager role. At the time I was a vice president and had been interviewing for roles at the senior vice president level, in positions that reported directly to the CEO. At this very large tech company, I would report into a director, who reported into a vice president, who reported into a senior vice president, who reported into the chief administrative officer, who reported into the chief operating officer, who reported into the CEO. This did not sit well with me, as I was very effective in influencing senior management teams on DEI strategy and processes and did not want to move to a mainly execution role in middle management. I did a bit of research and sent the recruiter a spreadsheet with 10 of their last hires in human resources, what their previous titles and responsibilities were, and what their titles were at the big tech company. All of them were at the director level, none at senior manager. All of them had nearly identical responsibilities and coverage as my existing role. And all of them were white. The recruiter pushed back and noted that I had limited experience managing global teams, despite the fact that I did have global coverage in my existing role. When I inquired about what that perceived gap meant in terms of the new job's responsibilities, she did not provide an answer. Do I think that recruiter was racist? No. Do I think one of the world's most respected tech companies is racist? No. Do I think this big tech company probably had a policy to under-level new recruits to the lowest position they might tolerate as part of some new organizational design policy to reduce the top heaviness of the company? Yes. And do I believe that candidates of color were the unfortunate victims of that scheme? Yes.

My story is but one anecdote, but far too often I hear from professionals of color their conviction that they have been under-leveled in their company. I hear this in courtesy interviews I do with Black, Hispanic/Latine, Indigenous, and Asian American employees. I hear it from these same types of professionals when they are candidates on our searches. They ask the critical questions about whom the role reports to and what the qualifications are of their peers in the function or business unit. And sometimes I have to have a tough conversation with a client when I believe a candidate we are presenting might be potentially under-leveled in the organization.

This issue is a big concern in the tech sector, in particular. Under-leveling results in a longer path to promotion to senior management.

It means that, over time, professionals of color show up with a less strategic, less impressive body of work when they compete and interview for senior roles in their current organizations or with potential new employers. And in the tech industry, where a big chunk of your compensation comes in equity and that equity is more lucrative the more senior you are in the organization, we are talking about potentially hundreds of thousands of dollars lost because of under-leveling. Other factors like a critical loss of confidence, diminished engagement as an employee, and low retention are important to consider as well.

In my opinion, however, the missed value creation that occurs when professionals of color are under-leveled is the biggest shame of all. It's like having Serena Williams play on the amateur circuit because the USTA doesn't think she's ready for Wimbledon. How tragic would that be? It happens in corporate America and in organizations of many shapes and sizes every day.

PART III

SOLUTIONS

POMEGRANATE PRINCIPLES

There are preexisting and some newly developing structural issues with the talent market and there are likely a few things you are doing at your organization that thwart your diversity recruiting strategies. There is still a lot in your control, however, if you want to achieve sustainable diversity recruiting outcomes. I want to share some principles I have learned over my 20-plus year career in executive search and DEI strategy development so that you can begin to lay a foundation to bring in diverse talent and reap the rewards of it. These principles represent many of the best practices I have seen implemented successfully at our clients, as well as some of the initiatives put in place at organizations known for innovative DEI strategies. Put together, these principles represent what an organization might implement if they truly are trying to maximize their chances at recruiting diverse talent the way a Phase Four company might.

CHAPTER EIGHT

PRINCIPLE 1: Building a Diverse Talent Pipeline in Advance of Hiring Needs

Companies and organizations that consistently produce diverse slates and consistently have success recruiting diverse talent almost never start from scratch with sourcing diverse candidates. They begin building a diverse talent pipeline well in advance of their hiring needs. There are a few successful tactics that I have seen companies and organizations employ to make sure they always have both diversity and liquidity in their candidate pipelines.

I am going to start with helping an organization in a difficult scenario: a Phase One company that does not have a track record of recruiting diverse talent, or one that is trying, but is struggling mightily, to do so. The strategy of building a diverse talent pipeline starts by building some initial awareness of your company and organization and to continue parallel processing other more specific outreach and employer branding efforts within these communities.

When it comes to building a diverse talent pipeline, the first thing to do is to start telling your story within communities of color. And the easiest way to do that is to find a compelling narrative about some element of your organizational culture that might resonate in professional communities of color. I know what you are thinking: we are in the agribusiness/cloud computing/pharma business and there is not really a narrative here. Every time I hear that from a client—and I hear it often—I typically can, based on the moderate amount of diligence I have done on that client, improvise a narrative that might be compelling to diverse professional talent.

For instance, I worked with a toy manufacturer on a senior-level legal search. The general counsel, a middle-aged white man, was my day-to-day client. I was going through my customary due diligence questions and asking about the number of attorneys of color currently working in the legal department. He proudly noted that there were three Black women working on the *Black Panther* movie project via a complex, multi-million-dollar licensing deal. I asked him if he had ever promoted this work in trade press, and he said no and hinted that he might not have ever even thought about it. I mentioned that I was fairly certain that *Black Enterprise, Savoy,* and *Essence,* three Black business and general interest publications, would be interested in a story titled: "The Women of Wakanda: The Attorneys Behind the Mega Licensing Deal with Marvel." I could almost see the lightbulb go on over my client's head. Although he had never thought about promoting a story like this, he instantly understood the benefits. He would be publicly applauding the hard work of a few of the stars on his legal team and sending a strong signal that people like them—Black women executives—were finding tremendous professional success at the company. Such low-hanging fruit might not only do wonders for the company's recruiting efforts, but it would go a long way toward retaining those women. You tend to think twice about leaving a job where your boss promotes your excellent work, your friends and work colleagues pat you on the back about the innovative projects you manage, and Big Mamma has the picture and article about you framed at her house for everyone to see during Thanksgiving.

Understanding and developing your enterprise's narrative starts with corralling your communications team and brainstorming all of the assets you have in terms of untold stories about the incredible work your diverse talent does at the company. If you can't find any employees of color to brag about, find a vendor in your supply chain. Interview them and ask them what the commercial relationship with your company means to them and to their employees. If you can't find a vendor, look through your charitable contributions and see if there is an Asian American, Black, Hispanic/ Latine, LGBTQ, or Indigenous organization you have partnered with recently, and ask about the same impact. Still nothing? Hire a diversity consultant and talk about your business or service model or mission and engage them to find out the implications for communities of color.

After you have established and promoted one or more direct narratives based on employees, vendors, or other stakeholders, it is time to scale and think about how you can show up in communities of color smartly on a consistent basis. My professional advice is to start small and scale appropriately. The next step might be inviting professionals of color inside your company for small, intimate meet-and-greets with company staff and leadership. After all, you now have one or more narratives about the great work your diverse employees or vendors or philanthropic partners are doing. It is time to tell that story directly through small, live curated events at your workplace. Inviting professionals of color inside your organization to talk and pose questions about the impact of your work on people or communities of color makes these stories vivid and memorable like magical realism in a great novel. You would be surprised to know how many companies do not do this and instead opt to do a talent/recruiting fair without much exciting content at the center of the event. Remember that first-generation big-time (FGBT) talent wants to know they can find purpose and meaning with their work, and it is likely your company has a good or even great story to tell.

I once hosted events like this at a company I worked for, and we were at capacity every single time. Furthermore, once word got out that we were hosting events with executives of color giving firsthand accounts of their career achievements at the company, I began getting invited to organizations to tell our company's story at other universities and POC professional/leadership development organizations. You do not necessarily have to promote open roles at your company at these events. In fact, it is better to host these events regardless of whether you have current unfilled roles. You are not hosting these events to fill jobs; you are hosting these events to tell your company's story to diverse audiences.

To be precisely prescriptive, this is what such an event looks like. You invite a diverse group of cross-functional professionals from the company to discuss their careers or the impact of new product or service lines on communities of color. These professionals span the entire company. You might have one or two people who are entry-level professionals in functional areas like legal/finance/marketing; two executives who are middle management (director or senior director level); and maybe one executive at management level (VP level). I would not advise having too many C-suite leaders as their presence tends to stifle open and frank discussion about the company.

Four people make for a great panel, as it does not require anyone to speak too frequently. An ideal panel might be to have two early-career professionals and two mid-career leaders. Each employee has a buddy, and they can riff off of each other during the panel. Ask the chief diversity officer or head of human resources or head of talent acquisition to host and moderate the discussion. If the topic is about the impact of the company's product or service or philanthropic contributions on communities of color, then invite the executives responsible for that project to host the panel and make sure to staff it with company employees who are familiar with the initiative. You can find a multipurpose room at your company or, if that is not possible, host it at a local college with significant students of color in their business school. It might make the company's staff more comfortable to host on-site, and it might provide a great window into the world of your company's culture to have your new guests see inside your offices, especially if they are branded and impressive.

These curated events are not just parties or receptions, however; they are sessions where you are telling your organization's story, capturing the interest of diverse talent, and mining information about them. I see a lot of companies dropping the ball on the follow-through from these events because they do not have a system to capture, categorize, and communicate with any of the dynamic professionals they meet at these events. Almost every applicant tracking system (ATS) has a way to capture talent for future follow-up. It is not the technology's fault when hiring managers or recruiters don't follow up with talent that they meet at these events. The real culprit is that most recruiters are overworked and understaffed and do not have time to do intentional follow-up and outreach to prospective talent. They can barely manage the existing requisitions they have. Recruiting teams are almost always staffed leanly because HR does not want to allocate too much headcount to talent acquisition, only to fire them during a downturn. I personally think it is great to park this responsibility with your chief diversity officer or, if you don't have one, with a dedicated employee in recruiting, or, if you can't commit to that, hire an external consultant to manage this project. The follow-up can be as simple as a quarterly call with each interested candidate to find out what they want to do in their next role, compensation expectations, and other factors you likely could not find out in a group event, but that you would find out during an interview process.

What you can do with just that information is pretty amazing. Just with knowledge of the person's career goals and compensation expectations, you can place that information in context of current or future openings at your company or consider them in a succession planning context. Instead of trying to bolt diverse talent onto the end of a recruiting process—something companies routinely do with almost always unsuccessful outcomes— sourcing diverse talent in advance of your needs does a few things to help hiring managers improve their efforts to recruit diverse talent over the long term. Now that I have outlined how to source diverse talent consistently over time, let's cover why this works to help actually recruit these leaders to your company or organization.

First, sourcing diverse talent helps you put professionals of color in play for roles that might not come up through the normal recruiting processes. I have worked in recruiting for over 20 years, so I know that not every open role advertised on the company's website is a "jump ball," an open, fair, and transparent process for any and all candidates. It is rare that when a VP leaves the company, the SVP has no idea who he or she might hire as their replacement. In most cases, the hiring manager knows whether he or she has bench strength to promote a director into that VP role, or whether that VP role can be combined with another VP's portfolio. Hiring managers do not often think through those succession opportunities with a lens for diversity unless it is strongly encouraged by HR and DEI leaders. Having a crop of diverse professionals pre-sourced allows you to consider those candidates for these kinds of roles when they come up.

Second, sourcing diverse talent helps you expand what you think about in terms of successful archetypes for the role. If your unconscious mind as a hiring manager skews toward thinking that an accomplished finance leader looks tall and white and male, your mind expands a bit when she is short and Latina. Why is this important? Because it takes time for anyone to reconsider preconceived notions of what leadership success looks like. And this is almost impossible to do within the throes of a recruiting process. Hiring managers are under tremendous time constraints and, if they are fortunate, they have a half dozen or more candidates to interview for senior director or VP-level roles. Their minds operate in a crucible of efficiency. I honestly do not think that most hiring managers are racist. But I do believe that bias creeps in as a convenient and unintentional shorthand for them to make low-risk decisions. Just like you need to experience the benefit of pomegranates over a period of weeks or months, being exposed to talented professionals of color in advance of an open role can literally change a hiring manager's mind about what the ideal candidate looks like, expanding it beyond the apples and oranges in the market.

Third, and related to the second point above, sourcing diverse talent in advance helps hiring managers understand that the pathway of POC talent is typically a different pathway than what you are used to with white candidates in corporate America. It may mean that your diverse candidates went to an HBCU, or a Hispanic/Latine-serving university. It may mean that they grew up in a certain part of the country, maybe more urban than rural. It may mean that their way up in their career may have been up the rough side of the mountain and they have had to scramble and fight to get to where they are. They may or may not go from Harvard to Goldman Sachs or from Yale to JP Morgan Chase—they may have had to really hustle and network and prove their value along the way, because they were not given the benefit of the doubt. You may learn that these different pathways that diverse talent take to get to the precipice of corporate leadership are very different paths from white candidates. Understanding the pathway of diverse talent may challenge your assumptions about what the "right" pattern is, or what the "right" pathway is to corporate or nonprofit leadership. This shift in the mentality of hiring managers means candidates of color look less risky over the long term. At scale, this shift can result in hundreds or thousands of candidates of color getting a first or second interview and possibly getting hired.

What you are also essentially doing when you reach out to diverse talent in advance is expanding the actual time of the sourcing process. Instead of saying to yourself, "Well, I have 90 days to recruit for this role," you have started a bit of a preseason round by having these events in your organization to get people familiar with your company. And the most important thing about that is creating some learning for your enterprise, for your diversity team, and talent acquisition and HR. Why do people of color lean into your organization as a potential new employer? Was it because of your healthcare benefits? Because you have amazing, industry-leading AI technology? Why did that young African American lean into your company? Was it because the CEO went to Dillard University, an HBCU? Or because you made a big contribution to the NAACP when George Floyd was murdered? Why did that Hispanic senior executive lean into what you are doing? Is it because you have a long-standing relationship with a

Hispanic-leaning university, and you have recruited from that school for 10 years? Understanding and constantly refreshing this narrative can help you create a compelling value proposition within diverse talent networks.

Yet another reason why building a diverse talent pipeline works is because it offsets the casual and even sometimes formal employee candidate referral process that helps populate candidate slates at companies and organizations. At tech companies, in particular, hiring managers often rely heavily on employee referrals for candidates. Here again, the need for speed dictates the recruiting methodology. It is certainly reasonable to expect current employees to be able to analyze organizational culture and understand who in their networks might have the skills, experiences, and temperament to succeed in the company. It is also reasonable to conclude that some employees are simply hooking up their smart and talented friends with jobs at a cool, high-growth or pre-IPO company with sky-high compensation and extraordinary benefits.

It is also reasonable to conclude that employees are recruiting people whom they are biased toward. I once led a tech startup, and I recruited the first five members of the team. They were all Black men, smart, ethical, and preppy, just like me. Our company was successful, but nowhere near the success we had hoped. Was my failed recruiting process to blame? It certainly played a part. That is not to say that these five people were not extraordinarily talented professionals. The problem was with me: I did not truly understand what the business needed, so I just hired people I knew and trusted.

This happens thousands of times in hundreds of companies. Most managers recommend and hire people who are proximate to them. Mark Zuckerberg knocked on the nearby dorm room doors at Harvard to find the first employees at Facebook. I called old classmates to find the first few employees at my startup. Neither Zuckerberg nor I spent considerable time trying to find the absolute best talent. There is no evidence, for instance, that Zuckerberg tried to recruit the best computer science graduates from nearby MIT versus his dorm door-knocking strategy. I certainly never asked my fiancée (now wife), then an MBA student at the University of Georgia, for any candidate referrals. This kind of informal, proximate talent sourcing process evolves into an employee referral system when a company scales, and it brings with it the same inconsistency and biases. To hedge against this inconsistency and bias, hiring managers must intentionally source diverse talent in advance of organizational needs by strategically looking far and wide for the absolute best talent. This can be a powerfully effective and equalizing factor for talent pipeline development.

The best compliment a Black preacher can pay to a white politician visiting their church is to say to their congregation that the candidate "doesn't just come around during an election." In the same way, a recruiter should go to the source of talent long before he or she needs to hire from it. With an even modest attempt, you will almost certainly find short-term success in recruiting leaders of color to your organization if you build a diverse talent pipeline in advance of your needs. Don't just wait until there is an open role. Discover your narrative assets. Tell your story within communities of color via events at your organization or at venues where the talent gathers. Promote stories about your diverse stakeholders in trade press and publications serving communities of color. Connect with diverse talent on a consistent and ongoing basis. Applying these techniques can disrupt some existing sourcing processes, which may be unintentionally thwarting opportunities for diverse talent to get careful consideration at your company or organization.

In other words, there is never a shortage of pomegranates if you stock up in advance.

CHAPTER NINE

PRINCIPLE 2: Expanding the Archetype of the Ideal Candidate

The second Pomegranate Principle is to expand the archetype of a successful candidate. One thing I see a lot of is companies and organizations getting into trouble when hiring managers start thinking, "I know who this person is," as they consider the ideal profile for a role. Many times, hiring managers base that conclusion on assumptions about what worked with a previous executive who served in that role.

For example, in an executive search, a hiring manager will try to maximize the chances of hiring the right candidate by noting that a particular candidate has industry experience, or that they are at a certain seniority level, or maybe they live in the same geography as the hiring company. The hiring manager will draw conclusions about a person based on the school they graduated from. I have had clients say to me, "Oh, I know who this person is. They went to Stanford, then to Cal Tech and they probably worked in the Bay Area for five different tech companies. They are ready to now lead this function." How do you know that candidate is the right person? You don't know, you can't possibly know the person by a quick review of a résumé. What you have done is articulate what makes you *comfortable* in making the selection, but there is no guarantee that the person you have selected will work out. They just fit an archetype that makes you feel comfortable.

I am not saying that this initial framing of a candidate is completely without merit. Most hiring managers are good-to-great evaluators of talent. The problem is their narrow framing of the archetype. Hiring managers typically look at what worked with the last most successful person in the role. That executive may, in fact, have been tremendously successful during a previous period. But it is very likely there are new stakeholders, new disruptions, new business or service lines or programs within the current incarnation of the company or organization. How is that previous leader's success relevant in this new era? It is like saying the United States needs a president like FDR to confront a world war and a depression when neither of those threats might face the country now.

Expanding the archetype means being open to nontraditional candidates. That becomes much easier if you have built a diverse talent pipeline because then you have exposure to profiles that challenge the existing archetype of the ideal candidate. You will be able to say, "Hey, you know what? The chief technology officer that I met at our meet-and-greet happens to be a Hispanic woman and she has a very different profile than Bill, our (white) chief technology officer. She's doing an incredible job at one of our competitors. And even though she doesn't have the same educational background or industry background as Bill, she's doing some amazing work." As you start expanding your archetype of what the role looks like, you will free yourself up to source diverse talent, and basically evaluate them through a different lens. If you have an expansive archetype, you will know that there is not just one type of candidate who can be successful at your company. You will be able to avoid limiting yourself unnecessarily to a narrow band of candidates.

An example of an expansive archetype is what President Obama did in his candidacy for U.S. president. Nothing he did, none of his qualifications fit the typical expectation of what a president is, or what qualities a president should have. He started a new archetype because, prior to Obama's election, the political pundits said you can't win the presidency if you are from the north. He was from Chicago. They said you cannot win the presidency if you are not an executive in government, most notably as a governor. Obama was a senator. The conventional wisdom was that you couldn't win the presidency if you do not have a military background. He had not served in the military. Furthermore, a candidate who acknowledged that he had smoked marijuana, had been in an interracial relationship, and had lived in Indonesia did not fit the prototypical presidential candidate.

Obama was a completely different archetype: a community organizer, civil rights lawyer, state legislator, and first-term U.S. senator. Most glaringly of course, Barack Hussein Obama was a biracial American without an Anglo-Saxon name. As a successful two-term president, Obama profoundly expanded the archetype of what a president looked like, sounded like, and what their personal and professional backgrounds could be. Today there are thousands of young Black and brown people (and white people, too) who say, "I'm going to work in social justice, and I want to be the president of the United States." Before Obama, that was never a path to being president.

Expanding the archetype does not mean that you water down or dilute the criteria. It means you understand there are different pathways to get to a great candidate and other organizations have solved this in different ways than you might have solved it. It means that your assumptions about what predicts success in the role might be dated and based on the last successful leader who faced a different set of stakeholders and challenges. Expanding the archetype means you understand that excellence comes in many different varieties. It means approaching the recruiting process differently. It means talking with recruiters and hiring managers who are interviewing candidates and influencing them to be open to candidates who may not have a traditional background. Expanding the archetype can be extremely helpful in getting a truly diverse slate of candidates.

Regardless of one's political views, it might be obvious in retrospect to understand why Obama was elected twice to the U.S. presidency. He was an inspirational orator with a visionary message ("Yes we can!"), moderate policies, a squeaky-clean personal and professional life, and he ran a scandal-free administration. Yet and still, I vividly remember debating with six big search firm recruiters who were certain that Obama would lose and, if he did win, would be a spectacular failure. When pressed about the reasons supporting both arguments, they cited the same reasons noted above: he did not have the government or military experience required to win or succeed as president. I did not (and still do not) think these recruiters were racist. I think they had a critical failure of imagination. They could not see possibility in Obama because the conventional wisdom blocked their vision of what could be. This competency—the capacity to recognize value and impact that others might miss—not only separates good recruiters from great ones, but I also believe it separates disruptive and transformational business leaders from the mediocre, unimaginative stewards of industry- and mission-driven organizations.

CHAPTER TEN

PRINCIPLE 3: Diversifying the Recruiting Process

Well-intentioned companies and organizations often look for the single magic elixir that can change their outcomes in diversity recruiting for the better and for the long term. Many have turned to the Rooney Rule, the NFL's initiative to require one person of color on every candidate slate for head coach and offensive and defensive coordinator roles. There is a lot of literature about whether the Rooney Rule works or does not work or whether it could ever work as currently configured. What I can share as someone who has worked with companies and sports clubs trying to implement the Rooney Rule is that no single recruiting technique will change the outcome of a search. This is why I am outlining these Pomegranate Principles, because a single technique is insufficient to transform such a complex and nuanced process as inclusive recruiting. One of the most powerful methodologies, which is really a set of processes under one rubric, is to diversify the entire recruiting process.

The first thing to diversify is the talent acquisition/recruiting team. This is important for three reasons. First, candidates of color tend to trust recruiters of color to tell the truth about whether a company or organization is a great place to work for professionals of color. It does not mean that white recruiters cannot empathize, engage, or otherwise connect with candidates of color. It means that if you want to maximize your chances of landing that passively interested candidate of color, having someone on the recruiting team who likely has some cultural aspects in common with them goes a long way.

Second, a recruiter of color also can help explain to hiring managers certain nuances on the résumés of professionals of color or contextualize certain attributes of candidates. If, for instance, a candidate attended Morehouse College and pledged Alpha Phi Alpha or attended Howard University and pledged Delta Sigma Theta, that accomplishment might be missed by a white recruiter, but be contextualized effectively by a Black one. It might be assumed that the candidate attended Morehouse or Howard—HBCUs—because they didn't get into Stanford or Princeton, when there are thousands of Black students who every year turn down elite, predominantly white institutions (PWIs) for HBCUs. Moreover, a white recruiter might not recognize that pledging (equivalent to being tapped or punched for a white fraternity or sorority) one of the Divine Nine fraternities or sororities at Morehouse or Howard means a less than 10% acceptance rate in some cases. As a recruiter, I look for credentialing with candidates through as many sources as possible. I'm looking to find where this person has passed through a rigorous, qualitative screening process. McKinsey & Company and Goldman Sachs provide one kind of credentialing. Student government, community service organizations, honor societies, and Black fraternities and sororities provide another kind as well.

A third value a recruiter of color can provide is to contextualize the behavior of candidates of color. I have a protégé who is phenomenally talented, creative, and tenacious. He also comes across as low key. He has gotten feedback about this from supervisors throughout his career and I am guessing from hiring managers and recruiters, too. I once had to defend him to a fellow senior executive at a company where we all worked. My senior colleague took his low-key persona as someone who did not get excited about new initiatives and who did not project passion to clients about their mission. I pulled this young Black male up and asked him about this. I mentioned that my white peer found him lacking energy, while I found him enthusiastic, resourceful, and creative during our work engagements. After our conversation, it dawned on me what the issue was: his cool persona as a Black male. My protégé wanted to come across as cool and always in control. I took no offense by this persona as I had seen it before and sometimes projected it myself. But my white colleagues saw someone uncaring and dispassionate. My protégé was anything but that, but viewed through different cultural lenses, his Black and white supervisors saw two different professional personalities.

Similarly, I have seen my white clients conclude that a candidate of color was not direct enough, not forceful enough, or not someone who could bust through walls by force of their personality. I had one client, a partner at a prominent venture capital firm, almost disqualify an incredibly accomplished executive because, in his opinion, the candidate did not have a take-charge personality. I told my client that this Black executive had been in consensus-driven environments as a partner and so he never had the professional opportunity to exhibit a command-and-control persona. Furthermore, I advised my client that Black male executives are scarcely afforded the same kind of leeway that white male executives have in terms of coming across as powerful, forceful executives. Think I'm wrong? Think of any Black male CEO—President Barack Obama; General Colin Powell as head of the U.S. military; Ken Chenault as CEO of American Express; Ken Frazier as CEO of Merck; or any other Black male CEO—and what persona comes to mind? A mild-mannered, nonthreatening, poised, and calm professional. There is not much room and there has never been much room for a pound-the-table FDR, Jack Welch–like persona for Black male leaders in corporate America. And I think the same is true for virtually all leaders of color. Few make it very far with dominant, forceful personalities. Having a recruiting professional on your team who can contextualize this can help you, as a recruiting manager, avoid passing on great candidates because they don't meet the Jack Welch test.

I once interviewed an executive for the deputy general counsel role at a large tech company. I was confident I had found a great candidate on an otherwise excellent and diverse candidate slate. He was a general counsel of a smaller, publicly traded consumer retail company with two degrees from Ivy League universities. I called a classmate of his from Harvard Law School and asked about his overall reputation and heard an exceedingly positive earful about his reputation and track record. Before this Black male candidate interviewed at the company, my client expressed considerable excitement about this candidate and his upcoming interviews.

I could hardly wait until our status call when we would hear feedback about the candidates who interviewed that week and the new prospects for discussion. My client was direct: the candidate we were both excited about would not be moving forward in the process. She explained that the culture of the company was one where executives and staff tend to vigorously argue out matters in meetings and that he seemed too soft spoken to thrive in their culture. "We're a pound-the-table kind of company, Rory; I don't think he'd survive too long here," she said. When I provided that feedback to the candidate, he was not surprised by it, which surprised me. He told me that, as a 6-foot-3-inch dark-skinned Black man, he had long ago learned he couldn't pound the table to make his point. "I have to be the black teddy bear, Rory, and I'm okay with that," he sighed. I could not convince my client that this was an unfair and exclusionary way of evaluating this candidate's fit for this role ("Is there a place for someone at the company who doesn't pound the table, but makes their arguments with a softer, but still data-driven approach?" I asked). I believe I likely would have been successful in convincing the recruiter had she been a person of color or there had been another person on the client side who was a person of color who could have chimed in on this matter. I think this particular trait among Black executives would have been contextualized and understood, and his candidacy might have survived beyond the first round of interviews. But his soft-spoken persona was seen as a defect immediately, and his candidacy was doomed fairly quickly.

Another area to diversify is the interview team, the staff who actually are going to meet and interview the candidates being considered for the role. Sometimes staff recruiters do not work through the entirety of the recruiting process. Some organizations have their recruiters focus on sourcing candidates and maybe staying engaged through the first round of interviews. Or maybe they get involved superficially in the recruiting process and miss out on the hugely important moments when candidacies are vulnerable: after the first- and second-round interviews and at the offer stage. Recruiters are rarely there for the actual interviews, which tend to be one-on-one meetings or panel formats with peer executives at the company or organization. For that reason, it is important to have a person of color on the interview team if you want to maximize your chances of creating and sustaining a diverse slate of candidates.

Diversifying the interview team is important for two reasons. One, a peer leader on the interview team can help influence the groupthink that tends to happen with interview teams or search committees. And it is very important that this person be a peer of those he or she is trying to influence. The opinions of internal recruiters, who tend to be junior or mid-level professionals, are sometimes dismissed simply because they are not peers of the executives interviewing candidates for a critical leadership role. Recruiters tend to have extremely valuable insights, but these insights sometimes get left on the editing room floor of the recruiting process. I have witnessed executives of color on search committees push back on the following comments and observations made by their fellow interviewers about candidates during the search process:

- That a candidate was in an interracial marriage and that might not play well within the organization.
- That a candidate, an Asian American immigrant, had a thick accent that might turn off stakeholders.
- That a candidate was too old to lead an organization with younger staff.

Without a peer executive challenging their reasoning and bias, some interview team members might have simply made bad hiring decisions. Taken alone, age, race, gender, or status in an interracial marriage are not only on the borderline of illegality and inappropriate to consider when evaluating candidates, they are simply bad data. None of that criteria regarding a person's status actually determines success in a role, yet those biased frameworks are used many times to disqualify candidates.

The second important reason to have an executive of color on the interview team is to help cultivate a close relationship with candidates of color interviewing for the role. A thought bubble over almost every candidate of color I have ever interviewed for a leadership role, in addition to questions about salary, growth trajectory of the enterprise, chemistry within the senior leadership team, and other usual topics, is this: What is it like for people like me at this organization? As an experienced executive recruiter, I try to get at this topic early in my own due diligence about the client during our kickoff call. I will often have a one-on-one with a senior leader of color at that organization and ask the tough and awkward questions. Is this is a fair organization for professionals of color? Are people of color respected within the culture? Are the CEO and senior leadership team truly committed to DEI? Having a sherpa who has a similar cultural background to a candidate of color can help build that much-needed trust at those critical stages of the recruiting process. Our firm, Protégé Search, has 10 consultants: five men and five women. I cannot imagine not having an ethnically diverse and gender-balanced recruiting team. We could never serve our clients effectively with all men or all African American recruiters because we could never build close relationships with candidates of color. I think that we at Protégé Search share the same perspective that executive leaders of color have when they serve on search committees or interview teams: the candidacies of executives of color must be managed with trust, care, and authenticity.

For example, I have a friend who was director of fundraising for a hospital system but was also the board chair of the NAACP. She was fairly early in her career, in her early thirties. Imagine the leadership potential and capacity she has in leading the nation's oldest and most revered civil rights organization as board chair, and how some of that leadership potential is not manifested in her day job in the hospital system. Somebody familiar with the responsibility of that volunteer leadership activity might tell a recruiter for the client, "Do you know what it takes to manage the board of directors of the NAACP?" and be able to translate that in her job there is a serious, complex influencing role that requires an amazing amount of emotional intelligence and savvy. It might mean that if, in reading her résumé, a recruiter only focused on her full-time employment positions, they might miss the tremendous leadership skills on display through her volunteer work. I fervently believe that professionals do not have résumés like this by accident because I have seen thousands of candidates like this in my recruiting career. I believe these types of résumés exist because these ambitious FGBT professionals of color are going to find ways to deploy their tremendous talent and skills by any means necessary. It might come via their church, a civic organization like The Links or The Boulé, or a fraternity or sorority. The experiences matter the same way being student body president in college matters alongside a high GPA. Diversifying the interview team means getting people from your company who can not only translate what is on a candidate's résumé, but deconstruct all of the relevant experiences in the candidate's background that might predict success in the new role.

Another benefit of diversifying the interview team is to help close candidates at the end of the search process. The period when a candidate gets an offer, but before they accept it, is a very vulnerable part of the search process. The candidate may ask, "What is my career advancement going to be like as a lesbian Latina?" If it is all white men on the interview team, what are they going to say? "I think it's going to be great"? But do they know that it is great for LGBTQ women of color, or do they just think that it is great for them as white men? They might be just giving the candidate some boiler-plate perspective about the generic leadership opportunities at the company, but what the candidate needs to hear is what it is like there as an LGBTQ woman of color from somebody who may actually understand what their career will be like at the company.

This example leads to another salient point: understanding that leaders of color are not a monolith. I have had friends tell me that they want to recommend a mutual friend to their company, but then tell me, "Our company will eat them alive." Why is that? It's often because a person of color with a similar personality didn't work out at the company and they fear rejection of an applicant who reminds them of that person. If you serve on the interview team, it's important in these cases to treat candidates as individuals and not racial representative samples. With a diverse interview team, you begin to better understand all of those nuances about the candidate pool, all of those relevant and impressive activities on résumés, and you have a deeper, more accurate understanding about individual candidates.

Also, if you interview together, you are less likely to have executives asking off-the-record questions. For example, when I was looking at a summer associate experience in law school, there was a very infamous example of a Chicago-based law firm where a partner, in an effort to test the mettle of one of the women candidates, said, "I want to ask you a question to get a sense of how you would deal with our fairly conservative culture. How would you respond if someone called you a 'nigger bitch'?" That probably doesn't happen if there is a Black woman next to the partner during the interview. (After an investigation, this particular law firm, at the time the biggest in the world, was banned from interviewing at the top-ten law schools for a decade.)

I have also witnessed men on search committees express caution about hiring a woman executive because of their concern about the woman taking time away to be with children. In addition to being an exclusionary and misogynistic tactic and very likely borderline illegal, these concerns are almost always unfounded by the facts. The male spouses of these women many times were taking primary care of the children, or the children were away at boarding school. Again, I do not and should not have to convey that information to push back on these opinions, but I find it dismaying that in 2023 people still think men and women occupy these fixed roles within their families. With a diverse interview team everyone behaves, I think, to a median level of polite, nonbiased questioning because there is a governor of someone from a different race or gender or sexual orientation sitting right next to you.

There is also a fair bit of complexity that goes into analyzing résumés of candidates, and having a woman or person of color on the interview team can help contextualize certain career transitions you find on candidate résumés. For instance, one candidate's résumé might show a series of 2- to 3-year stints in the early part of their career over three or four roles in various cities until the person has a 5- or 6-year stint at one company in the middle part of their career. Another candidate's résumé might show four 6-year stints where the executive was promoted twice in each role. One might naturally assume that the second candidate has the preferred career path with the longer stints and promotions. But what if the other candidate had a trailing spouse and that required them to move every couple of years? What if that same candidate was sexually harassed or racially discriminated against by their supervisor on two of those occasions? These are the sensitive topics that women and people of color might understand based on their own experiences, and they might bring those perspectives into analyzing candidates' career paths. These are issues that we routinely talk about on our internal team calls at Protégé Search because we are constantly wading into the often nuanced career paths of women and executives of color. To not acknowledge these issues is to be blind to the real-world challenges facing women and people of color on their career journeys.

With a diverse recruiting and interview team, your company is ahead of many companies trying to recruit diverse talent. This puts you squarely in the Phase Two section of the DEI continuum outlined earlier. The two elements that almost all Phase Four companies have is sustainable diversity on candidate slates and a partnership with a diversity recruiting firm. Let's talk about how to get a diverse slate of candidates and how to achieve this consistently over time.

The first factor that predicts success in achieving a diverse slate of candidates is the capacity of your recruiting team, whether internal or external. I have witnessed this firsthand as a senior HR leader and as an external executive recruiter. Internal recruiters are most often incentivized by the time it takes to close on recruiting projects. The quicker they close a search, the better. The stress of "time to close" as your guiding mantra means that prioritizing speed with the recruiting process translates into using that recruiter's tried-and-true techniques for sourcing and qualifying candidates. Time to close does not allow for extensive or creative sourcing strategies. You start with whoever the usual suspects are for the role and try to persuade your internal client that one of those candidates fits the role. Internal recruiters also do not have the seniority or influence to push back on senior hiring managers. If a senior hiring manager does not seem to be particularly concerned about diversity, it is rare for a recruiter to advocate for DEI on their own. Without time to consider the fullness of the market of candidates or the leverage to push back on the "don't ask/don't tell" mentality of hiring managers about DEI, it is almost a guarantee that recruiters will underachieve on creating diverse slates. And if they do succeed at developing a diverse candidate, recruiters will many times put just one or two candidates of color on a slate of eight or more candidates. Research has shown that one candidate of color on a slate almost always gets "othered," isolated as a check-the-box candidate and becomes someone hiring managers consider too out of the box for serious evaluation.

The big search executive search firms don't help matters much. There are a few executive recruiters of color at the large international search firms who, in my opinion, are highly ethical and committed to DEI. But the truth is that a big search firm often thwarts these noble instincts. I spoke with one of the top executive recruiters in the country for Chief

Information Officers (CIOs). I asked him how it was possible that he billed $3 million every year in client fees. "How do you find time to find the right candidates every time?" I asked. He proudly touted "the list" of leaders he constantly sourced for searches and told me: "This is the list of the top 200 CIOs and the top 200 deputy CIOs in America; all I do is shuffle the profiles on this list for clients." As someone almost always sourcing brand-new candidates for my searches, I was awestruck, but somewhat depressed by this revelation. Here I was calling senior executives to get nominations for leaders of color, calling into African American, Hispanic/Latine, Indigenous, and Asian American professional development organizations, in addition to tapping into databases to build bespoke, diverse candidate slates, and this veteran recruiter already had the slate developed before the search began. Did his firm care about his laziness with candidate sourcing and his apathy about creating a diverse slate? I doubt it. As long as he billed $3 million and they took their $2 million, all was forgiven.

But what happens when a client does call a search firm out on the lack of diversity with the candidate slate? Most times, the search firm says, "We tried," and talks about the millions of profiles in the database and that, despite their best efforts, there simply are not any diverse candidates available for a role. And the client often takes that at face value. After all, this is a search firm that makes $500 million a year with offices all over the world. If they can't find diverse candidates, maybe they can't be found? That is just not the case. I remember being asked to join a brainstorming session in the legal practice at one of the big search firms. The practice leader hurriedly scheduled the call and explained that a client was holding the firm's feet to the fire about candidate diversity. He asked the six of us on the call whom we could recommend. I instantly chimed in and recommended an exceptionally qualified Fortune 500 securities attorney, who happened to be a friend and classmate from Harvard Law. "Where did you find him?

How do you know him?" the partner exclaimed, hoping that he had found the answer. "He's in the firm's database," I replied. As the partner and other practice members reviewed his résumé and background, they were all impressed, and the partner agreed to present him to the client.

I was not surprised to hear that my friend got the job. He relocated halfway across the country and was excited to start his new professional adventure. How was he, a Williams College and Harvard Law grad with big law firm and Fortune 500 legal experience, overlooked on the initial search? It is simple: the partner very likely submitted his usual suspects, some castoffs from previous searches, and candidates from his own "go-to list" of attorneys to the client. Even so, I don't think that partner is racist or even biased. Lazy? Yes. Unimaginative? Absolutely. But racist? I don't think so. But I do think that big search firms are incentivized just like internal recruiters to close searches as quickly and as efficiently as possible. In that way big search firms are like big restaurant chains. The goal of the firm is to ensure a level of quality across all of its operating branches. Just like Morton's Steakhouse wants your steak in Miami to taste as good as it does in Las Vegas, the big search firms are trying for commercial consistency, not creativity. I tell our clients that Protégé Search is more like a farm-to-table restaurant. We only have one "office," and our goal is to provide a uniquely creative and special experience. We know our clients come to us because they already have been to Morton's, and they want something a bit more distinctive.

A partnership with a diversity recruiting boutique likely is going to be a distinctive and beneficial experience for your diversity recruiting efforts, whether it is Protégé Search or one of the many other firms in our sector. That is likely for three reasons.

First, any diversity recruiting firm worth their salt is going to have a brand and a level of trust within the community of professionals of color that big search firms will not be able to match. That is because we are not simply managing a niche professional services business, but we live within, socialize within, and network within a broad set of professional communities. As of this writing, I split my time between Lisbon, Portugal, where my child attends high school, and Potomac, Maryland. I am either grabbing dinner with entrepreneurs, attorneys, investors, and tech leaders in Lisbon, Paris, Amsterdam, Berlin, and other cities I travel to for work and leisure in Europe, or I am in DC, New York, Seattle, San Francisco, New Orleans, or other U.S. cities visiting with candidates and clients. I am the recent past president of the Harvard Law Black Alumni Network and a resident of a golf club community in Potomac, Maryland, where my family is one of a few Black families in our neighborhood. My social life is a mixture of white, Black, Asian American, Hispanic/Latine, Indigenous, LGBTQ, veterans, and people with disabilities. I did not engineer my social life to mirror my professional life; my career was built around my social and professional networks. These overlapping communities between my career and my social networks are much more dynamic and robust now that I am leading a diversity recruiting firm. I was told over and over again in my career that there wasn't any money in diversity recruiting. When I made a literal business case for this to be my professional focus I was counseled by many senior leaders that diversity did not translate into money. While I may have had some overlap in my career and personal networks 15 years ago, I was in no way incentivized to build and cultivate those networks.

Now, those professional and social networks pay big dividends for our executive search clients. I am able to get nominations for positions quickly and hear firsthand experiences from those who have worked with candidates we are pursuing for our clients. I have asked for recommendations for candidates for searches while walking on the beach in Martha's Vineyard. I have been at house parties and gotten an earful from a friend about a candidate and why they might have been eager to get out of their current organization. I have met sources and candidates and clients at Black film festivals, diversity-themed golf tournaments, cycling tours in France, fraternity events, HBCU homecomings, and other events with a broad cross-section of diverse professionals.

The second reason that a diversity recruiting boutique likely is going to serve your company better than a big search firm is that the small search firm owned by an entrepreneur of color cannot afford for the search to fail. At big search firms, many routinely build a 20% failure rate into their search practice. That means if you, as a consultant at the firm, need to close 10 searches a year to be eligible for a bonus, it means you need to have worked on 13 searches over the year. Searches cancel for a variety of reasons, including the client no longer having the funding for that role; the client going through a company-wide hiring freeze; the client losing faith in the search firm's ability to successfully complete the search; and for a few other reasons. Some clients fire search firms because they do not produce diverse slates of candidates. I know, because a good 50% of our work comes from companies and nonprofits that have fired a big search firm for failing to heed their need for diverse slates of candidates. And when that big search firm fails the diverse slate test, what happens to the consultants working on those searches? From my experience, not much happens. It is just chalked up within the 20% failure rate and everyone moves on. A diversity recruiting firm cannot afford to not create diverse slates, let alone get fired for it. Just like any small professional services firm with dozens, but not thousands of clients, each client matters more. There is simply more at risk for a small recruiting agency if they get a search wrong, and that incentive is a powerful motivator to get it right.

The third reason a diversity recruiting firm is a potentially good partnership for your company or organization is perhaps unique to Protégé Search: we actively strive to help our clients do diversity recruiting as well as we do. We recognize that we are not going to get every search from a client; executive search is a pricey solution, and most companies use search firms only when they have to. Our goal at Protégé Search is to give each client the benefit of our decades of working with clients across sectors and in almost every function so they can apply these techniques themselves. This phenomenon is actually the impetus for me writing this book: to share diversity recruiting best practices at scale, rather than on a client-by-client basis. I tell our team at Protégé that we are truly adding value once we start helping a client apply diversity recruiting strategies across their enterprise and not just on the searches we are working on at the moment. In that way, the fee a client pays us gets them the diversity recruiting service on a particular search, but also a significant amount of DEI advisory services. In addition to sharing these diversity recruiting strategies, for free or at cost, I have also done the following for clients:

- Shared the principles and strategies in this book, which originated as a 90-minute webinar on diversity recruiting best practices for hiring managers.
- Provided group career coaching for ERGs focused on employees of color.
- Provided executive coaching for the executives we place with our clients.

Simply put, you are going to get more value for your money, you are going to learn much more about diversity recruiting, and your company likely is going to be able to apply best practices in diversity recruiting going forward and be much more self-sufficient in your future talent acquisition needs if you use a diversity recruiting firm like ours. For those reasons, a partnership with a diversity recruiting firm could be transformational for your organization's diversity recruiting outcomes.

CHAPTER ELEVEN

PRINCIPLE 4: Recruiting the Whole Person

Recruiting the whole person is not the most significant Pomegranate Principle, since all the strategies of the framework need to work together seamlessly, but it is the one principle that is often overlooked by companies or is dismissed as not important. The issue that many companies find themselves in is this: if it is true that people typically quit their jobs because of a bad boss, they also leave companies because they do not like the overall environment of the organization and its physical geography. They can't bring their whole lives to that organization. They can't authentically live the life they want in a particular city or the overall setting—the company plus the geography. I had a client that lost a candidate of color because that person said, "I can't live in this city. I love the role. I love working at this organization. I love my team, but I haven't been able to bring my social life from Atlanta to Seattle." And this candidate left and there was nothing the company could do. They can't pay him enough. They can't promote him enough. They can't give him a senior enough role. If this person cannot find a social, cultural, spiritual, or educational environment that sticks with him and his lifestyle and his family, he is not going to stay at the company. And if he can't work remotely, he will take another job in a geography more amenable to his quality of life. It is why I am a big advocate for remote work to improve DEI recruiting outcomes. If all of Silicon Valley allowed for remote work, and Black and Hispanic/Latine and Indigenous professionals could work from Los Angeles, Houston, Atlanta, and Chicago, the number of available candidates of color would skyrocket.

The issue of being able to bring your full self to a new geography is something I understand completely because I experienced this as a candidate. I interviewed at a tech company in California, and at the time I was working on the East Coast. The company was a well-respected big tech company and the entire recruitment process involved recruiters and executives at the company telling me how great a fit I would be for their organization and what a great company it was. They talked about all the innovation in their product and service lines and what they were going to roll out in the future and how I would be a big part of their success moving forward. It didn't work out in the end because I couldn't bring my Black life to the Bay Area in California. I couldn't find a neighborhood that was diverse. I couldn't find a school system that was diverse. I couldn't find a golf club that was diverse. I couldn't find any of the other cultural elements that tethered me to a community. All I was going to have was a cool job, but that was not going to be enough to keep me there. Yes, I might move there and yes, it may be so much compensation that I stay there, but eventually I am going to be looking over my shoulder, trying to get back to Washington DC, Atlanta, Chicago, Houston, or Los Angeles— trying to get back to places where there is great diversity and great social and cultural infrastructure for me to keep my personal life engaging. This may not be an issue that impacts candidates of color all the time; we have recruited candidates from a variety of backgrounds to Seattle, for instance, who left thriving social lives behind and endeavored to build new ones in the Pacific Northwest. My experience suggests, however, that it matters to a significant percentage of candidates of color, and hiring managers need to consider this issue early in the recruiting process.

My own experience is not an outlier but is something I hear from executives of color on a consistent basis. I had an executive coaching client who worked for a major aerospace company, and I mentioned earlier that the issue with him was that he didn't trust the organization, he didn't trust that he could take intellectual risks with his role and still be successful at the company. After our coaching assignment, he got put into a stretch assignment in South Carolina to be the communications and marketing director at a manufacturing plant. When I checked in with this person a month or two into it, he said, "This is really, really tough. It's tough on my family because my kids are now in a public school, and they are not being welcomed that much by these white kids who see these new Black kids from out of town. They have been mistreated by them and the teachers are not exactly welcoming, either." And he continued, "Oh, and by the way, I've been stopped three times on the way to work or coming home from work in my BMW for no reason. I don't have a taillight out. I don't have a missing tag. I'm not speeding. I just pass in front of a police officer and when they see me, they stop me. And now I have this sort of Pavlovian notion every time I go to work and come home, and I have to think, 'Am I going to get stopped by the cops?' I come into work stressed and I leave work stressed."

I am guessing that the company never thought about that. I am guessing that they never thought that there would be a tax so high on this guy's family, that his kids would suffer in school and that he would be profiled by the police. They just thought, well, the job is amazing, and this is a great platform for you in your career. Had they thought about it carefully, if they really understood what it meant for an African American to move to South Carolina into that kind of community, they likely would have (or should have) reconsidered this particular locale for his stretch assignment. But the point is, they did not think about it. This executive had to maneuver through a scenario that he couldn't even talk about, couldn't even broach the topic with others at work. Obviously, the company does not bear any responsibility for what the teachers do to his kids and what other kids do to his kids and what the cops do to him. But they do bear some responsibility for understanding how these situations might affect his performance; they do need to understand how his external life might affect his engagement, understand how that might affect his retention as an employee. When another company calls him, as they did, and says, "Hey, I know you live in Texas and we're headquartered in Ohio but you can work remotely and stay in Texas," he jumps at the opportunity. It is not about money, it is about being able to live his life. He is closer to family and friends, and his kids don't have to change schools, move out of their house, and deal with a corporate apartment. He does not have to navigate through a new community, join a new church, or find people who share his hobbies. A lot of companies miss this point completely when hiring managers assume that relocation cuts across the candidate pool evenly and equally.

Knowing your environment, being comfortable in that, is hugely important to a person of color. They know the streets not to go down. They know the places around town that are pretty conservative. In a new city, they have to learn that all over again. Then there is the issue of law enforcement. Because racism does not fall equally in America, and law enforcement does not fall equally on America, and police profiling does not fall equally in America, you are asking someone to learn both the culture of your company and the culture of that community. Every Black man I know—and I am guessing the same is true for Hispanic or Latino men— has been stopped by the police. Many times, these stops are on the way to or on the way home from work.

It is always something we consider when recruiting diverse talent because it is our lived experience as Black and Hispanic/Latine and Indigenous and Asian American recruiters. I was stopped by the police near our home in Potomac, Maryland. I was speeding in my Audi trying to merge into a very short merging lane. As soon as I overtook the BMW that was not letting me merge, the patrol car stopped me. The first thing that popped into my mind was whether our will had been finalized. I recognized that this experience could be life or death for me. The white male police officer could not have been more courteous and let me off with a warning. When I got home and told the story to my wife and child, they both said, almost in unison, that the experience likely would have been very different had I been stopped in Virginia or Prince George's County. Montgomery County officers were considered the most friendly in the metro area. How many recruiters or hiring managers at companies research the relative police profiling in their cities versus the cities where their recruits of color are relocating from? I am guessing the answer is somewhere between zero and very few.

There are other important cultural considerations when a professional of color relocates. Transplanted professionals of color have to relearn how to create safe spaces in a new community. Where can they get their hair cut or braided or styled? Where can they find ethnically relevant hair-care products and makeup and facial creams? Where can they find soul food or ethnic grocery stores? What neighborhoods can they go to? Who is a good realtor for people of color? It is almost like you have to imagine the person of color is going to a foreign country as an expat because, in some parts of America, the challenges of being accepted in these social and business networks and neighborhoods are that significant.

What we do in the recruiting process at Protégé is we find out early on the quality-of-life requirements for the candidate in the case of a relocation. Are they on corporate or nonprofit boards in their local community? Are they actively involved with their son or daughter's baseball or basketball team? Are they active in their fraternity or sorority or prestigious and exclusive civic and social organizations? Do they have a barber or hair stylist whom they finally found who keeps their appointment times? Some of the answers to these questions are revealed through the multiple conversations we have with candidates. I know that if, for instance, a professional is very active in their community through nonprofit advocacy organizations or professional development groups like The Links, The Boulé, or a fraternity or sorority, it is going to take a compelling narrative to get them to relocate. They are not only active in their community, but these organizations provide a social and emotional bulwark against the challenges of working in complex organizations, especially large companies and nonprofits.

Why is this important element of the search process overlooked? I think there are two reasons. One, I think hiring managers simply assume that because they love Austin, Boston, or Seattle, candidates of color will love it too, and for the same reasons. The antidote to this is to ask people of color in your organization at the same professional level what they like or don't like about the city and what they wished they knew before they relocated there. That might provide hiring managers and recruiters with some nuanced perspective about what it takes to close that leader of color you want to recruit.

The second reason I think this strategy of recruiting the whole person is overlooked is that hiring managers are nervous about asking personal questions of candidates. You can get into dicey legal territory asking candidates if they are married or how many kids they have. Those are not only problematic and likely illegal questions to ask, but they do not get to the information you need. Again, protected class status questions yield bad data. It is perfectly okay, however, to ask a candidate how they like living in their current city and if they have any questions or concerns about relocating to the new city. And it is also perfectly okay to ask a similarly situated leader of color inside your organization to help you answer any questions that the candidate asks. By thoughtfully considering the whole set of circumstances surrounding your recruit's candidacy, you can stay ahead of the competition and successfully close on them for that open role.

CHAPTER TWELVE

PRINCIPLE 5: Onboarding Diverse Talent

The retention of an executive begins in the recruiting process. And the best way to retain a professional or executive of color is to create the conditions in which they can do their best work. That starts immediately after they have accepted the offer to join your company. What expectations were set during the recruiting process? What alignment is there between what the enterprise needs and what this person can deliver? What resources were promised and are those promises actually kept? If you promise a candidate something about budgets or headcount or reporting relationships, fulfilling those promises is critical to building trust. Any misalignment, any gaps not covered during the recruiting process, leave open a space where uncertainty can creep in. It allows a candidate who may be relocating or entering a new industry to be that much more rattled as they settle into their new role. And if they cannot trust the company to keep promises they made when the candidate's leverage was sky-high as a finalist on a search, what will happen once they join the company and get into the throes of their work?

There are things companies can do to offset that, to put that uncertainty to rest. The first good thing you want to happen, the optimal thing you want to happen, is for this person to get off to a fast start. You want them to build relationships with the key stakeholders inside the company whom they need to influence and impress, and you want them to put up a win or two. It could be a listening tour, it could be a strategy plan, it could be something else, but in the first 90 days, you want to be able to report that your new recruit is doing fabulously well. During those spontaneous water-cooler conversations when you are asked, "How's Jamal doing?" you will be able to respond, "Oh, he organized and led the town hall meeting. He's doing great." And when you are asked, "How's Vinita doing?" you will be able to say, "Oh, she managed that big conference we had with our vendors. She's doing great." You want to be able to state something palpable to other people in the organization who ask about the new executive you have hired, because one of the ways in which people get derailed in their new roles is when the early reviews are neutral to negative. "Hey, how's Keisha doing?" and you respond, "You know, it's too early to tell," or you respond with the real career-breaker, "It's mixed." It is very hard for any new recruit to bounce back from bad feedback in the first 90 days.

And the reason that it is so important to get new talent off to a fast start by putting up some wins is that there are always stakeholders—some supportive and some skeptical—observing them over their first few months. There is always a jury of people watching and scrutinizing, and it might not be just the people in your department; it may be people adjacent who collaborate with you. It may be direct reports. It may be the person who was an internal candidate who did not get the job. There is always a jury of skeptics when you join an organization and both the new person and the manager who hired them want to be able to put those skeptics at bay by getting the new executive off to a fast and successful start.

While helping your new executive get on track to secure some early wins is the low-hanging fruit over the first 90 days, the second thing you want to happen is to avoid harming or damaging that person's confidence. If a person of color arrives anywhere near the C-suite, it is very likely, as I have noted before, they have run a gauntlet to get there. In the game of Corporate Survivor, they did not take a limousine to the finish line. They had to battle every person on the way up the mountain, overcome every obstacle and hurdle thrown their way. They had little food or water, and they had to take a bus, sleep outside, and then walk another 20 miles before, finally, arriving at the finish line of the C-suite along with everybody else. That person has a unique confidence, one borne from being resourceful, from being effective in dealing with less and achieving a lot without the requisite professional and social networks you typically need to succeed.

What I have seen happen at a lot of companies is that the organization unintentionally destroys the confidence of their new hire. The typical way in which confidence is destroyed is by giving a person an initial high-profile assignment, but not providing cover as their boss. The problem is thinking, "Oh wow, this person worked at GE and Goldman Sachs so surely I can throw them into this very complicated assignment with all of these important stakeholders and they'll be just fine." Not necessarily. Not because they do not have the technical expertise, but because they do not know that the CFO focuses only on the financials in the decks and if they are not perfect in that regard, they will pay a price. And the CMO expects all of the go-to-market metrics to be accurate and the presentation to be very polished. And don't forget the COO—she is a stickler for institutional memory and the history of the organization. All these unwritten rules are things your boss should obviously know. But if your new recruit does not navigate the first 30 to 90 days with that kind of nuance, they likely are going to raise some doubts among the skeptics. Before long, their reputation will be that their performance is "mixed," the corporate kiss of death.

Mixed. I hate that word. I have heard that word used to describe a professional of color who a white supervisor thought was not performing up to par. I have heard it used to describe employees who were truly screwing up in their jobs, and I have heard it used to describe employees who were actually performing excellently in their roles. In other words, I have almost never heard it used accurately. It is as if white managers are mindful about characterizing the performance of professionals of color too harshly, lest they be accused of racism. So, they have to find a word that signals what they mean without sounding too damning. I sometimes think senior leaders must have some passive-aggressive lexicon they use to signal a whole lot of meaning in a single word or phrase. *Mixed* is one of them. "Too aggressive," "not substantive enough," and "not a culture fit" are a few of the other phrases of death for a professional of color. Describing leaders of color with these terms slowly starts their demise at their new employer.

If the talent you just spent months recruiting appears to not "get it," whatever "it" is in terms of the culture in your organization, they will get off to a slow start. It's not just a bad scenario because it harms the person's reputation; it's a bad scenario because the feedback is often so vague that the person doesn't know how to course correct. And so they take fewer risks and play defense as a professional. The employee, the team, and the enterprise suffer as a result. They put their tail between their legs, they try to make sure they don't screw up further, and they take easy projects. And over the course of the next year, year-and-a-half, they don't have a body of work that is impressive. They are playing defense because all they are doing is trying not to get fired. It is like a tennis player trying to avoid a double fault on their serve. They are trying to avoid that penalty that came to them during the first 90 days from happening again.

Again, the twin existential threats to newly hired diverse talent are not putting the person in a position to succeed in their first 90 days and damaging their confidence early on. And the solution to both threats is to simply help the person get off to a fast start, help them put up some wins in the organization by providing an assignment or project that their boss shepherds and stewards to minimize the risk of that project going sideways. And then it is important to proselytize their success inside the organization when it does go well.

Another important thing to do is to identify a sponsor for your new recruit. A sponsor, not a mentor. The difference between a mentor and a sponsor is that a mentor speaks *to* the professional about their career, and a sponsor speaks *about* the professional to powerful and influential people inside the organization. This is something that should be lined up during the recruiting process before the person actually takes the job. That effusive praise the general counsel made about the controller candidate during the search process? Leverage that to get her to be a sponsor for the new recruit.

A great sponsor should do the following for their protégé:

- Provide a perspective about other C-suite leaders.
- Help broker introductions to other influential leaders inside and outside the organization.
- Provide institutional history about the organization.
- Serve as an evangelist to trumpet the success of their protégé.
- Provide transparent and constructive feedback about their performance (if observed).

It is so important to get this sponsor/protégé relationship established in the first 90 days. I remember earlier in my career the powerful benefits of having sponsors. At one company, I had two of them and they each helped me in different ways. One helped me understand the very complicated politics inside the organization, who had power and who did not, whom I needed to curry favor with, and whom I could ignore and roll my eyes about behind their back. He was also an incredible institutional historian about the organization and could caution me before I went down a particular path. My other sponsor was simply a bullhorn for my hard work and achievements. I would get emails from powerful executives at the company that they heard about something I did, and they would offer congratulations. Almost always the positive word was first spread by this sponsor. Imagine my peers who did not have that. Maybe they are doing great work, but nobody knows about it. I have been that person, too. I was nearly fired from my job because a supervisor had it out for me for some reason and began to poison the well about my reputation. Luckily, I had a late developing sponsor who pushed back on my perceived negative reputation. A great sponsor is a great insurance policy for your recruit, so identify them as early as possible.

Of course, there are other important things to do with your new recruit that many companies fail to do in the onboarding process. Some of them are so easy that I cringe when friends and colleagues call me to complain about how awkward their onboarding has been. Here are some simple things to do to help your new recruit get off to a fast start:

- Pronounce their name correctly and email everyone about the pronunciation.
- If they are a person of color and your organization is not that diverse, make sure security and the front desk personnel know when their first day of work will be. (Do I need to share the story of the chief diversity officer at the big tech company who was stopped and harassed by security on their first day of work?)
- Send them some company swag. Polos, water bottles, and backpacks are a nice touch. If you are a consumer brand with cool products, sending your new recruit something exclusive is an even nicer touch.
- If staff work on-site in the office, take them out to lunch on their first day and out to drinks (if they drink) at the end of their first week.
- If possible, have them deliver a presentation to an influential internal or external audience within the first 90 days.

We are such big believers in the importance of onboarding diverse talent that we offer executive coaching for each of our placements as part of our search fee. It can be helpful to partner with our recruit's new employer to make sure they get off to that fast start. This can entail ensuring that the promises made during the recruiting process—things like reporting relationships, key strategy decks, invitations to speak or participate at company or external industry events—are followed through appropriately. It can include making introductions to peer executives in our network who are in similar roles. And it also could include more intensive coaching to help shore up a developing leadership competency with the placement candidate.

CONCLUSION:
What Else Can You Do?

I f you have read this far, you might come to the correct conclusion that it takes a lot to consistently succeed with diversity recruiting. You also may think that your organization is not prepared to invest in all of this infrastructure with DEI, that you do not have the funding or talent to achieve your diversity recruiting goals. That, too, may be correct. My goal with *The Pomegranate Principle* is not to demand that you immediately put in place the initiatives and processes of a Phase Four organization on the DEI spectrum; my goal is that you do something to move *toward* that end of the continuum.

So, what else can you do? There are three things a hiring manager can do immediately after you put this book down. First, you can share any DEI principles or techniques that you found intriguing with your colleagues in human resources, diversity and inclusion, or on the senior management team. That may spark a dialogue about what is working and what your organization has the capacity to try to implement on a pilot basis. It may, in fact, catalyze an audit of your DEI recruiting infrastructure to measure it against the organizational outcomes you desire.

Second, you can talk to a recent recruit who also happens to be a person of color and ask them about their experience as a candidate. What was their experience with the recruiting firm or with the internal recruiter? How was the interview process? Did they feel like they got their questions answered, both about the role and, if applicable, their relocation to a new city? How was their onboarding? Do they already have a sponsor and, if so, how is that relationship working out? I will go out on a limb and bet that few hiring managers consistently ask these follow-up questions during the first few weeks of the new hire's tenure.

Third, you can position yourself as a DEI advocate for the long term. Encourage your fellow hiring managers to have patience as your organization architects the diversity recruiting framework that will be built to last. Listen to their frustration and offer support when they hit an inevitable valley on their diversity recruiting journey; be the evangelist for a long-term approach to implementing these measures. Equal to the patience required to evolve your organization is the imagination required to move it forward on the DEI continuum. Promote the narrative that the best version of your company or organization is on the other side of this DEI journey. Help your colleagues imagine a more innovative, more resilient, and more collaborative organization when they get frustrated and reach for the old tropes about DEI being a compliance or check-the-box initiative.

Collaboration. Empathy. Imagination. These are foundational principles you can apply to achieving sustainable diversity recruiting outcomes wherever you are. These are also great values for all of us to live by, whether as leaders, citizens, or simply as human beings sharing this wonderfully imperfect, but redeemable world in which we find ourselves.

NOTES

CHAPTER 1

1. EDsmart. (2022). The Great Resignation statistics. https://www.edsmart.org/the-great-resignation-statistics/.
2. Burton, J. (2017). Largest growing segment of entrepreneurs in America. *Her Own Mind* (11 June). https://herownmind.com/largest-growing-segment-entrepreneurs-america/ and Cimini, K. (2020). 'Puro cash': Latinos are opening more small businesses than anyone else in the US. *USA Today* (23 May). https://www.usatoday.com/in-depth/news/nation/2020/02/24/latino-small-business-owners-becoming-economic-force-us/4748786002/.
3. Lean In. (2023). Women in the workplace study: The state of women in corporate America. https://leanin.org/women-in-the-workplace.
4. Solomon, O. (2022). 55% of Black Americans say they've never had a mentor. *Recruiting Daily* (6 June). https://recruitingdaily.com/news/55-of-black-americans-say-theyve-never-had-a-mentor/. Lean In. (2020). The state of Black women in Corporate America 2020. https://leanin.org/research/state-of-black-women-in-corporate-america/section-2-support-at-work.
5. Jobs for the Future. (2022). Survey reveals barriers that prevent Black workers from entering and advancing in tech careers. Press release (26 May). https://www.jff.org/what-we-do/impact-stories/jfflabs/survey-reveals-barriers-prevent-black-workers-entering-and-advancing-tech-careers/.
6. IBM Institute for Business Value. (2020). Untapped potential: The Hispanic talent advantage. IBM. https://www.ibm.com/thought-leadership/institute-business-value/en-us/report/hispanic-talent-advantage.

CHAPTER 2

1. Glenn, R. (2019). Charlie Sifford: A hard road to golf glory. USGA (3 February). https://www.usga.org/articles/2012/02/a-hard-road-to-golf-glory-2147484 5949.html#:~:text=Golf%20has%20long%20struggled%20with,from%20 competing%20on%20the%20PGA.
2. Goldstein, D., Grewal, M., Imose, R., and Williams, M. (2022). Unlocking the potential of chief diversity officers. McKinsey & Company (18 November). https:// www.mckinsey.com/capabilities/people-and-organizational-performance/our-insights/unlocking-the-potential-of-chief-diversity-officers.
3. U.S. Census Bureau. (2022). Quick facts: Population estimates July 1, 2022. https:// www.census.gov/quickfacts/fact/table/US/PST045222.
4. Stevens, P. (2020). Companies are making bold promises about greater diversity, but there's a long way to go. CNBC (15 June). https://www.cnbc.com/2020/06/11/ companies-are-making-bold-promises-about-greater-diversity-theres-a-long-way-to-go.html.

CHAPTER 7

1. McKinsey & Company. (2021). Race in the workplace: The Black experience in the U.S. private sector (21 February). https://www.mckinsey.com/featured-insights/ diversity-and-inclusion/race-in-the-workplace-the-black-experience-in-the-us-private-sector.

INDEX

Women in the Workplace Report
    (McKinsey & Compoany/
    LeanIn.org study), 25
Woods, Tiger, 41, 112
Work, avoidance (choice), 8
Workforce, Black workers
    (percentage), 111
Workplace culture

discussion, 15
fairness, 83–84
World Trade Center, terrorist attacks
    (impact), 75

Year of Return, 102

Zoom interview, interruption, 33